Fundamentals of C & Data Structures
A Beginners guide

AF426577

Dr. Ravikanth Motupalli
Dr Chalumuru Suresh
Dr. Appala Srinuvasu Muttipati

Copyright © 2023
All Rights Reserved.

This book has been self-published with all reasonable efforts taken to make the material error-free by the author. No part of this book shall be used, reproduced in any manner whatsoever without written permission from the author, except in the case of brief quotations embodied in critical articles and reviews.

The Author of this book is solely responsible and liable for its content including but not limited to the views, representations, descriptions, statements, information, opinions and references ["Content"]. The Content of this book shall not constitute or be construed or deemed to reflect the opinion or expression of the Publisher or Editor. Neither the Publisher nor Editor endorse or approve the Content of this book or guarantee the reliability, accuracy or completeness of the Content published herein and do not make any representations or warranties of any kind, express or implied, including but not limited to the implied warranties of merchantability, fitness for a particular purpose. The Publisher and Editor shall not be liable whatsoever for any errors, omissions, whether such errors or omissions result from negligence, accident, or any other cause or claims for loss or damages of any kind, including without limitation, indirect or consequential loss or damage arising out of use, inability to use, or about the reliability, accuracy or sufficiency of the information contained in this book.

Made with ❤ on the Notion Press Platform

www.notionpress.com

Contents

Foreword

It is with great pleasure that I introduce you to "Fundamentals of C & Data Structures," a comprehensive journey through the essence of programming and the intricacies of data manipulation. This textbook is carefully crafted to equip you with a profound understanding of C programming and the fundamental principles that govern data structures.

Chapter 1: Introduction to C Programming In this foundational chapter, readers are introduced to the fundamental principles of C programming. It provides a solid groundwork for understanding the syntax, structure, and basic concepts that form the backbone of the C language.

Chapter 2: Functions and Storage Classes Building upon the basics, Chapter 2 delves into the world of functions and storage classes. Readers explore the modular nature of functions and gain insights into the different storage classes that define variable lifetimes and scopes.

Chapter 3: Arrays, Pointers, and Strings This chapter explores the trio of essential data elements in C programming. Arrays, pointers, and strings are unravelled, showcasing their pivotal roles in organizing and manipulating data within a program.

Chapter 4: Structures and Unions introduces the concepts of structures and unions, illustrating how these constructs allow for the creation of complex data types. It explores the organized architecture of structures and the versatile overlays provided by unions.

Chapter 5: Files Diving into the external realm of data storage, this chapter focuses on file handling operations. Readers learn how to open, close, read, and write to files, gaining a crucial understanding of persistent data manipulation.

Chapter 6: Searching and Sorting Efficiency takes the spotlight in Chapter 6, where various searching and sorting algorithms are explored. From linear to binary searches, and bubble sort to quicksort, this chapter equips readers with the tools to organize and retrieve data optimally.

Chapter 7: Data Structures unfolds the realm of data structures. Readers delve into organized structures, pointers, and arrays, understanding their role in dynamic and efficient data handling. This chapter lays the foundation for more advanced data manipulation.

Chapter 8: Trees and Graph In the final chapter, the complexity deepens with an exploration of trees and graphs. Hierarchical structures and intricate relationships are unveiled, providing a comprehensive understanding of these fundamental data structures.

These chapters collectively guide readers through the essential concepts of C programming and data structures, paving the way for a holistic understanding of programming principles and practices.

Preface

In crafting the pages of "Fundamentals of C & Data Structures: Beginners Can Learn Easy," our intent is to create a welcoming gateway into the realm of computer programming and data organization. Recognizing that embarking on this journey can be both exhilarating and challenging, we have designed this book with the novice in mind, aspiring to make the complexities of C and data structures accessible to all. We embark on a pedagogical adventure, demystifying the intricacies of the C programming language, covering its essential elements from variables to file handling. Simultaneously, we guide beginners through the fundamental structures of data, such as arrays, linked lists, stacks, queues, trees, and graphs, with an emphasis on simplicity and hands-on learning. Through practical examples and a step-by-step approach, we aim to empower beginners, ensuring that each concept is not just understood but mastered. This book is an open invitation to the world of programming, where even the most inexperienced learners can take their first confident steps. Happy coding, and may your programming journey be both enlightening and enjoyable!

Within the pages of this book, we weave a narrative of discovery and growth, recognizing that the journey from a novice to a proficient coder is a series of small victories. As beginners navigate through the chapters, they'll find not just a manual, but a companion that nurtures curiosity and fosters a genuine understanding of programming fundamentals. The language is deliberately simple, the examples thoughtfully chosen, and the exercises strategically placed to reinforce learning. Our commitment is to demystify the seemingly complex world of C and data structures, making it an enjoyable expedition for those taking their first steps into the expansive universe of programming. May this book be the catalyst that transforms aspiring beginners into confident coders, ready to explore the limitless possibilities that the world of C and data structures has to offer? Happy coding, and may your programming endeavors be both enlightening and fulfilling!

Date

Acknowledgments

In expressing my heartfelt acknowledgment, I extend my deepest gratitude to the wonderful individuals who have played pivotal roles in bringing "Fundamentals of C & Data Structures: Beginners Can Learn Easy" to fruition. This book is not just a product of solitary effort, but a testament to the collaborative spirit of friends, supporting members, and the inspiring works of fellow authors.

To my friends, your unwavering support and camaraderie have been the bedrock of this endeavor. Your enthusiasm, late-night discussions, and invaluable feedback have infused this book with a sense of shared purpose and joy. Your belief in the project has been a constant source of motivation, and I am truly fortunate to have such a supportive circle.

A heartfelt thank you goes out to the supporting members, both directly and indirectly involved in the creation of this book. Your diverse skills, perspectives, and dedication have enriched the content and elevated it to new heights. This collaborative effort wouldn't have been the same without your collective commitment.

I also want to express my appreciation for the authors whose works have inspired and guided me throughout this writing journey. Your insights, wisdom, and mastery of the craft have left an indelible imprint on this book. It's an honor to stand on the shoulders of literary giants and contribute to the knowledge-sharing tradition.

To those authors whose books have been constant companions, thank you for sharing your expertise and passion for programming and data structures. Your influence is evident in the pages of this book, and I am grateful for the wealth of knowledge you've provided.

In conclusion, this book is a collaborative tapestry woven with the threads of friendship, support, and shared knowledge. Each contributor, in their unique way, has played a crucial role in the realization of this project. Thank you all for being an integral part of this journey, and I look forward to sharing the success of this book with this amazing community.

Prologue/Introduction

In setting the stage for "Fundamentals of C & Data Structures," our journey begins at the crossroads of logic and organization. This book, designed for those taking their inaugural steps into the realm of programming, is a beacon illuminating the pathways of the C programming language and the fundamental structures that shape the digital landscape.

As we venture into the prologue, envision a canvas waiting to be painted with the strokes of syntax and the elegance of data manipulation. C, a venerable language with a timeless appeal, becomes our linguistic brush, allowing us to craft programs that breathe life into machines. The journey doesn't stop there; it extends into the intricate world of data structures, where arrays, linked lists, stacks, queues, trees, and graphs become the architects of organized information.

This prologue is an invitation to curious minds eager to unravel the mysteries of coding and data organization. Through the following chapters, we embark on a deliberate exploration, demystifying complexities and laying a foundation for a lifelong journey into the intricate art of programming. Welcome to a world where code becomes poetry, and data structures orchestrate the symphony of digital logic. Let the journey into the fundamentals of C and data structures begin.

1. Introduction

Objective

1. Provides knowledge of algorithms and flowcharts.
2. Teaches how to structure C programming.
3. Enhances understanding of the concepts of tokens, variables, data types, and their respective sizes.
4. Covers control statements in C programming.

C programming, born in the early 1970s, stands as a testament to enduring excellence in the realm of computer programming. Its inception, rooted in the need for a versatile and powerful language, has paved the way for a legacy that continues to shape the foundations of software development. C is celebrated for its efficiency, portability, and direct access to the machine's hardware—qualities that have made it a language of choice for system programming and embedded systems.

At its core, C is a procedural programming language, emphasizing modularity and clear program structure. The simplicity of its syntax, coupled with its ability to provide low-level access to memory, empowers programmers to craft efficient and concise code. The language's influence extends beyond its own syntax; C has served as the inspiration for numerous programming languages, further solidifying its impact on the field.

As we delve into the world of C programming, this introduction marks the commencement of a journey into the language's fundamental elements. From data types and operators to control statements, each facet contributes to the elegance and power that defines C. Whether you are a seasoned developer or a newcomer to the coding landscape, the exploration of C programming promises insights into the essence of a language that continues to shape the digital landscape. Welcome to the journey of unraveling the intricacies and unlocking the potential of C programming.

Algorithm

Definition: An Algorithm is a step-by-step procedure to solve a given problem

An algorithm consists of a set of explicit and unambiguous finite steps which, when carried out for a given set of initial conditions, produce the corresponding output and terminate in a fixed amount of time. By unambiguity it is meant that each step should be defined precisely i.e., it should have only one meaning. This definition is further classified with some more features.

According to D.E.Knuth, a pioneer in the computer science discipline, an algorithm has five important features.

i) **Finiteness:** An algorithm terminates after a fixed number of steps.

ii) **Definiteness:** Each step of the algorithm is precisely defined, i.e., the actions to be carried out should be specified unambiguously.

iii) **Effectiveness:** All the operations used in the algorithm are basic (division, multiplication, comparison, etc.) and can be performed exactly in a fixed duration of time.

iv) **Input:** An algorithm has certain precise inputs, i.e. quantities, which are specified to it initially, before the execution of the algorithm begins.

v) **Output:** An algorithm has one or more outputs, that is, the results of operations that have a specified relation to the inputs.

Let us take some examples to illustrate all the features of an algorithm.

Example 1: Algorithm to find the sum of two numbers:
Step 1: Start
Step 2: Read two numbers
Step 3: Perform the sum of two numbers
Step 4: Print the sum
Step 5: Stop.

Example 2: Algorithm to find average of five numbers:
Step 1: Start
Step 2: Read first number
Step 3: Read next number
Step 4: Perform sum of the two numbers
Step 5: Repeat steps 3 and 4 until all the numbers are read
Step 6: Calculate average by dividing the sum with 5
Step 7: Print the average
Step 8: Stop.

Example 3: Algorithm to find the number of vowels in a given sentence:
Step 1: Start
Step 2: Set number of characters=0,number of vowels=0
Step 3: Read a character
Step 4: Add 1 to the number of characters
Step 5: If it is an vowel(a,e,i,o,u,A,E,I,O,U) then add 1 to the number of vowels
Step 6: Move to the next number
Step 7: Repeat steps 4,5 and 6 until all the characters are read
Step 8: Print the number of vowels
Step 9: Stop

Example 4: Algorithm to find largest of two numbers:
Step 1: Start
Step 2: Read two numbers A,B

Step 3: Compare A and B. If A>B, print A
Step 4: Else print B
Step 5: Stop.

Example 5: Algorithm to find largest of three numbers:
Step 1: Start
Step 2: Read three numbers A,B and C
Step 3: Compare A and B
Step 4: If A>B, then compare A and C else compare B and C
Step 5: If A>C, then print A
Step 6: If B>C, then print B
Step 7: Else print C
Step 8: Stop.

Example 6: Algorithm to find highest marks of student in a class:
Step 1: Start
Step 2: Read marks of first student
Step 3; Set highest=marks
Step 4; Read next student's marks
Step 5; Compare the marks in step 4 with the highest found marks so far
Step 6: If marks in step 4 > highest found marks, then make the marks in step 4 as highest
Step 7: Repeat steps 4,5 and 6 until all the students' marks are read
Step 8: Print the highest marks
Step 9: Stop.

Example 7: Algorithm to find the roots of a quadratic equation:
Step 1: Start
Step 2: Read a,b,c
Step 3: Find discriminant d=b2-4*a*c
Step 4: If d>0,
$$r1=(-b+\sqrt{d})/(2*a)$$
$$r2=(-b-\sqrt{d})/(2*a)$$
Step 5: Else if d=0,
$$r1=(-b)/(2*a)$$
$$r2=(-b)/(2*a)$$
Step 6: Else print roots are imaginary
Step 7: Stop

Example 8: Algorithm to print pass or fail message based on the average of 4 subjects marks:

Step 1: Start
Step 2: Read the marks of 1st subject
Step 3: Read marks of next subject
Step 4: Perform sum of 2 subjects marks
Step 5: Repeat steps 3 and 4 until all the marks are read
Step 6: Calculate the average by dividing the sum with 4
Step 7: If average>=50, print the message pass
Step 8: Else print fail
Step 9: Stop.

Example 9: Algorithm to find largest number from N numbers.

Step 1: Read N
Step 2: Large = 0,
Step 3: Count = 0
Step 4: Read num
Step 5: If num > Large then

    Large = num
Step 6: count = count +1
Step 7: If Count < N then   Goto step 4
Step 8: Print Large
Step 9: Stop

Example 10: Algorithm to find smallest number from two numbers.

Step 1: Read two numbers n1 and n2.
Step 2: If n1 < n2 then
    Small = n1
  else
    Small = n2
Step 3: Print Small
Step 4: Stop

Example 11: Algorithm to find smallest number from three numbers.

Step 1: Read three numbers n1, n2 and n3.
Step 2: If n1 < n2 and n1 < n3 then

                        Small = n1
          Else
               If n2 < n1 and n2 < n3 then
                       Small = n2
              else
                       Small = n3
Step 3: Print Small
Step 4: Stop

Example 12: Algorithm to find smallest number from N numbers.
      Step 1: Read N
      Step 2: Read Num
      Step 3: Small = Num
               Count = 1
      Step 4: Read Num
      Step 5: If Num < Small then
               Small = Num
      Step 6: Count = Count +1
      Step 7: If Count < N then   Goto step 4
      Step 8: Print Small
      Step 9: Stop

Example 13: Algorithm to find factorial of a given Number
      Step 1: Read N
      Step 2: Fact=1
      Step 3: Count = 1
      Step 4: Fact = Fact * Count
      Step 5: Count = Count +1
      Step 7: If Count < = N then   Goto step 4
      Step 8: Print Fact
      Step 9: Stop

Example 14: Algorithm to find sum of N positive integer numbers
      Step 1: Read N
      Step 2: Sum = 0,
      Step 3: Count = 0
      Step 4: Read Num
      Step 5: Sum=Sum + Num
      Step 6: count = count +1
      Step 7: If Count < N then   Goto step 4

Step 8: Print Sum
Step 9: Stop

Example 15: Algorithm to find GCD of two given numbers
Step 1: Read M,N
Step 2: temp = Remainder of M / N i.e. temp = M%N
Step 3: M=N
Step 4: N=temp
Step 5: if N > 0 then goto Step 2
Step 6: GCD = M
Step 7: Print GCD
Step 8: Stop

Example 16: Algorithm to find whether the given number is Prime Number
or not
Step 1: Read Num
Step 2: Prime = True
Step 3: I = 2
Step 4: Rem = Num % I
Step 5: If Rem = 0 then Prime =False
Step 6: I = I + 1
Step 7: If I < N then   Goto step 4
Step 8: If Prime = True then
                    Print Num is a prime number
            Else
                    Print Num is not a prime number
Step 9: Stop

Example 17: Algorithm to print Fibonacci series up to 15 terms
Step 1: Previous=0
            Present = 1
Step 2: Print Previous, Present
Step 3: Count = 2
Step 4: Next = Previous + Present
Step 5: Print Next
Step 6: Count = Count + 1
Step 7: Previous = Present
Step 8: Present = Next
Step 9: If Count < 15 then   Goto step 4
Step 10: Stop

Example 18: Algorithm to find Largest and Second Largest of
N numbers

       Step 1 : Read N
       Step 2: Large = 0, SecLarge = 0, Count = 0
       Step 3 : Read Num
       Step 4 : If Num > Large then
                   SecLarge = Large
                   Large = Num
          Else
                 If Num > SecLarge then
                 SecLarge = Num
       Step 5 : Count = Count + 1
       Step 6 : If Count < N then   Goto step 3
       Step 7 : Print Large , SecLarge
       Step 8 : Stop

Example 19: Algorithm to find the sum of digits of a given
integer number

       Step 1 : Read N
       Step 2: Sum = 0
       Step 3 : Digit = N % 10
       Step 4 : Sum = Sum + Digit
       Step 5 : N = N / 10
       Step 6 : If N > 0 then   Goto step 3
       Step 7 : Print Sum
       Step 8 : Stop

Example 20: Algorithm to find LCM of two given numbers
       Step 1: Read M, N
       Step 2: A = M,   B = N
       Step 3: Temp = M % N
       Step 4: M = N
       Step 5: N = Temp
       Step 6: if N > 0 then goto Step 2
       Step 7: GCD = M
       Step 8: LCM = A*B/GCD
       Step 9: Print LCM
       Step 10: Stop

Example 21: Algorithm to find total marks, average and result
of a student

```
Step 1 : Read  stno,m1,m2,m3
Step 2:  Tot=m1+m2+m3
Step 3 : Avg=tot/3
Step 4 : if  m1<35 or m2<35 or m3<35 then
                    Result = Fail
                    Else
                    Result = pass
Step 5 : Print Tot,Avg,Result
Step 6 : Stop
```

Program

A program is a set of instructions written in a programming language that directs a computer to perform a specific task or set of tasks. These instructions, known as code, are designed to be executed by the computer's central processing unit (CPU). Programs can range from simple scripts automating basic tasks to complex software applications with sophisticated functionalities. The process of creating a program involves writing human-readable code, which is then translated into machine-readable instructions through compilation or interpretation. Programs are the foundation of software and enable computers to perform a diverse array of functions, from calculations and data processing to running applications and managing hardware components.

There are many ways to solve most problems and also many solutions to most problems

Flowchart

The most difficult and important task within programming is the systematic and careful analysis of a whole problem. Therefore, before going to actual programming, a programmer should always go through the following steps in a sequential order.

   i)   Design an algorithm representing the process of solution of the problem.

   ii) Represent the algorithm through a flowchart for a better understanding of the algorithm.

iii) Code the flowchart i.e. write instructions in a programming language that a specific computer will accept.

iv) Run/Execute the program on the computer for the given data (Input) and get the output.

Flowcharting: Flowcharting is a graphical representation of an algorithm. The pictorial representation of the algorithm is called a flowchart. A flowchart is a picture, that shows the sequence in which data are read, Computing is performed, decisions are made and results are obtained. It makes use of the basic operations in programming. All symbols are connected among themselves to indicate the flow of information and processing.

i. **Terminal:** The oval represents any terminal point in a program and generally contains such words as BEGIN, START, END or STOP.

ii. **Input/Output:** The parallelogram represents the Input/Output function i.e. making data availiable for processing (input) or recording of the processed information (output). This step implies obtaining a number from an Input device (say, the keyboard and storing it in the storage location names 'A').

iii. **Process:** The rectangle represents the processing operation. A process changes or moves data. An assignment is normally represented by this symbol.

iv. **Flow direction:** Lines or arrows represent the flow direction function – the flow of control. Normal flow direction is from left to right or from top to bottom.

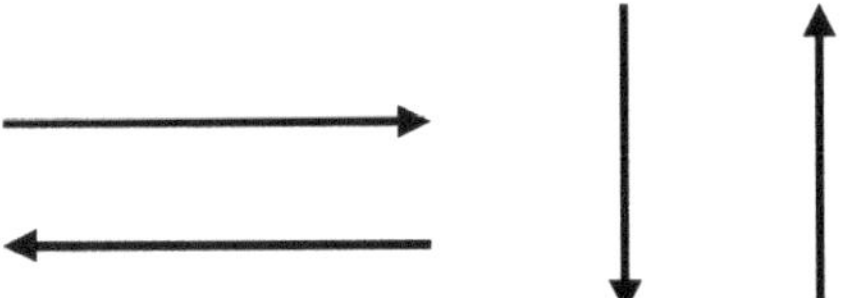

v. **Annotation:** A broken line and bracket represent the annotation function – the addition of descriptive comments or explanatory notes for clarification of some statements.

vi. **Decision-making symbol:** The diamond represents a decision or switching type of operation that determines which of the alternative paths is to be followed.

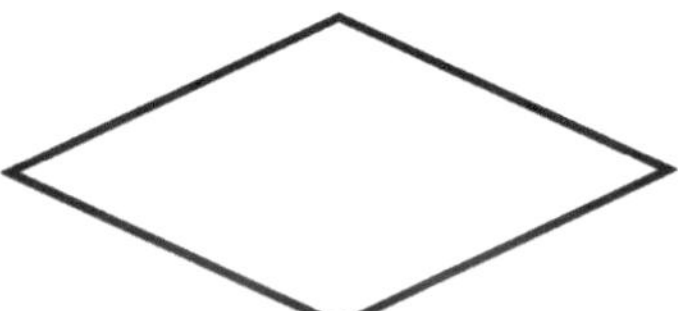

vii. **Connector:** The circle represents a function in a flow line.

viii. **Pre-defined process:** The double-sided rectangle represents a named process that consists of one or more operations or programming steps that are specified elsewhere, such as a module or subroutine. We will use these flowcharting symbols for representing algorithms.

Flowchart to print sum of two numbers

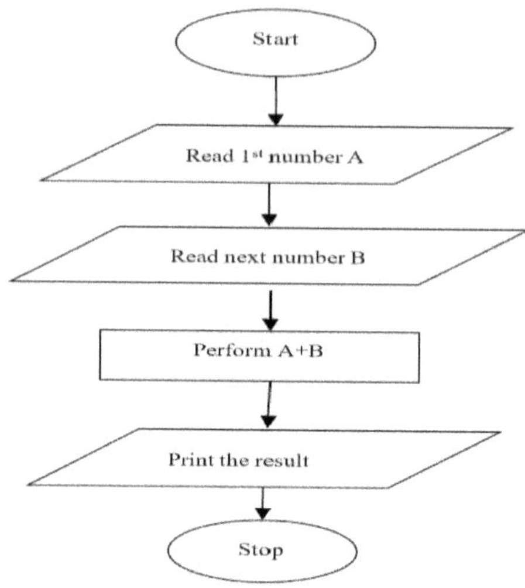

Flowchart to print average of five numbers

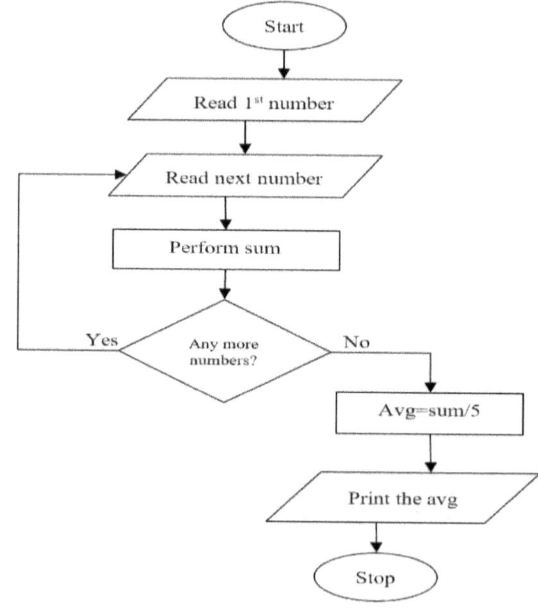

Flowchart to print the number of vowels in a sentence

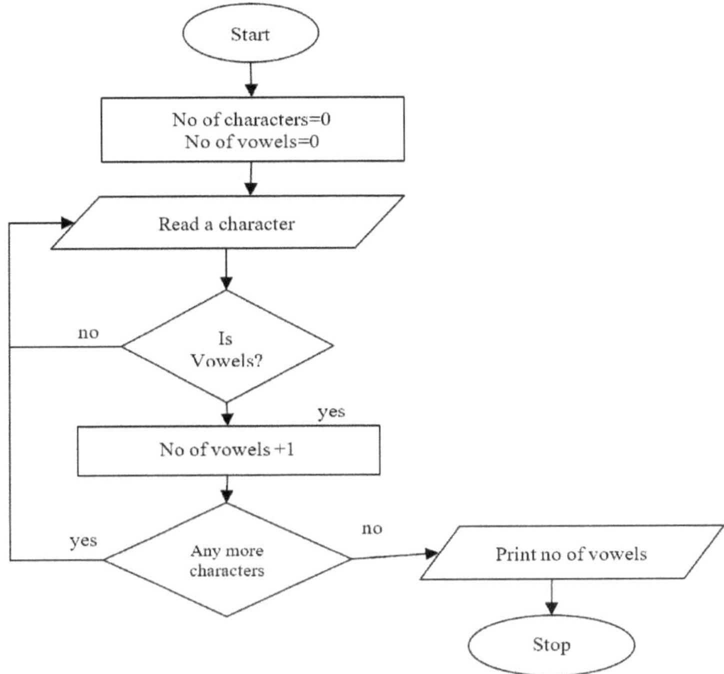

Flowchart to print the largest of two numbers

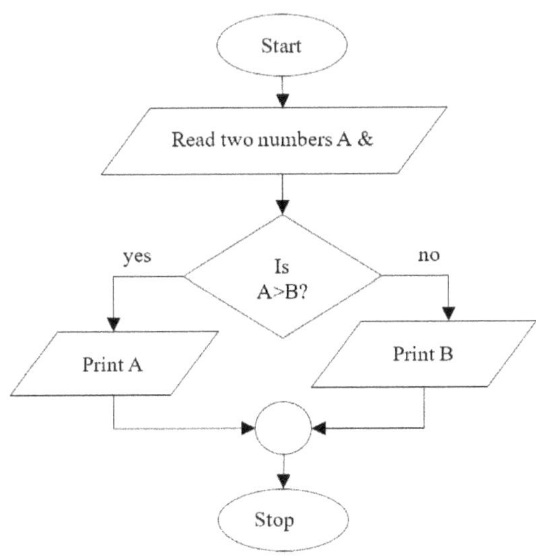

Flowchart to print the largest of three numbers

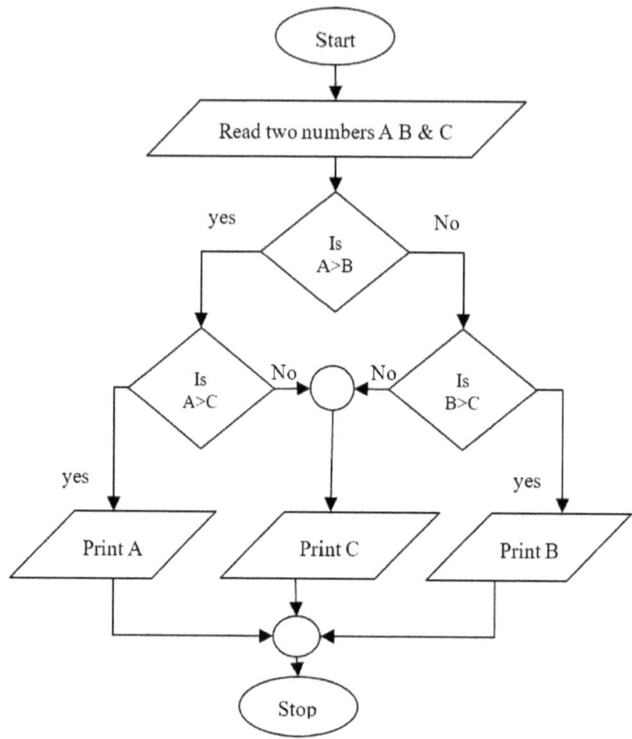

Flowchart to find largest of 2 numbers

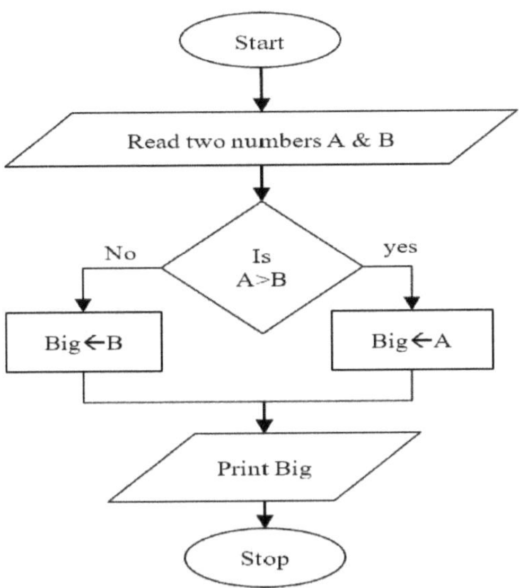

Flowchart to print the highest marks of student in a class

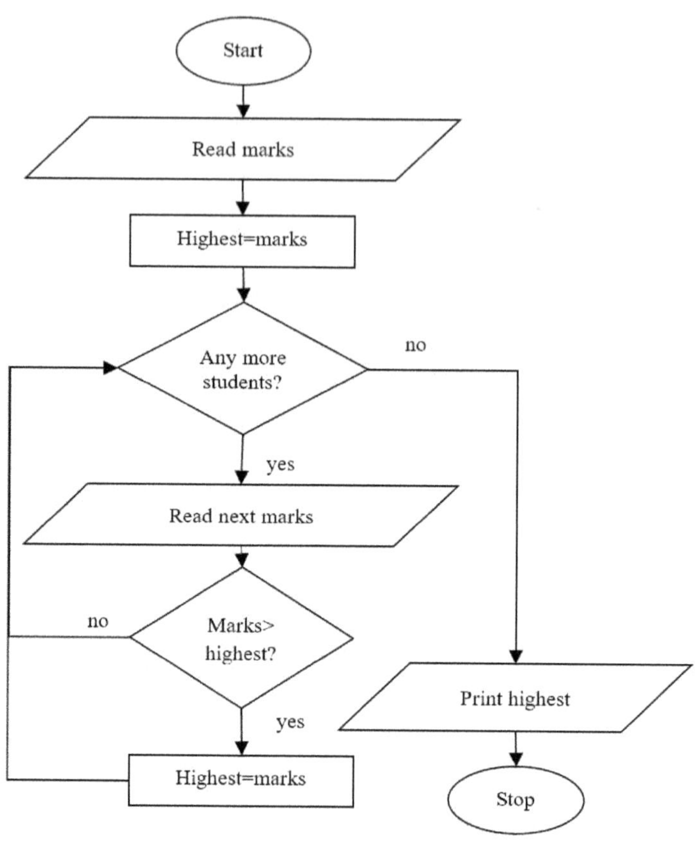

Start
Read marks
Highest=marks
Any more students?
no
yes
Read next marks
Marks> highest?
no
yes
Highest=marks
Print highest
Stop

Flowchart to print roots of a quadratic equation

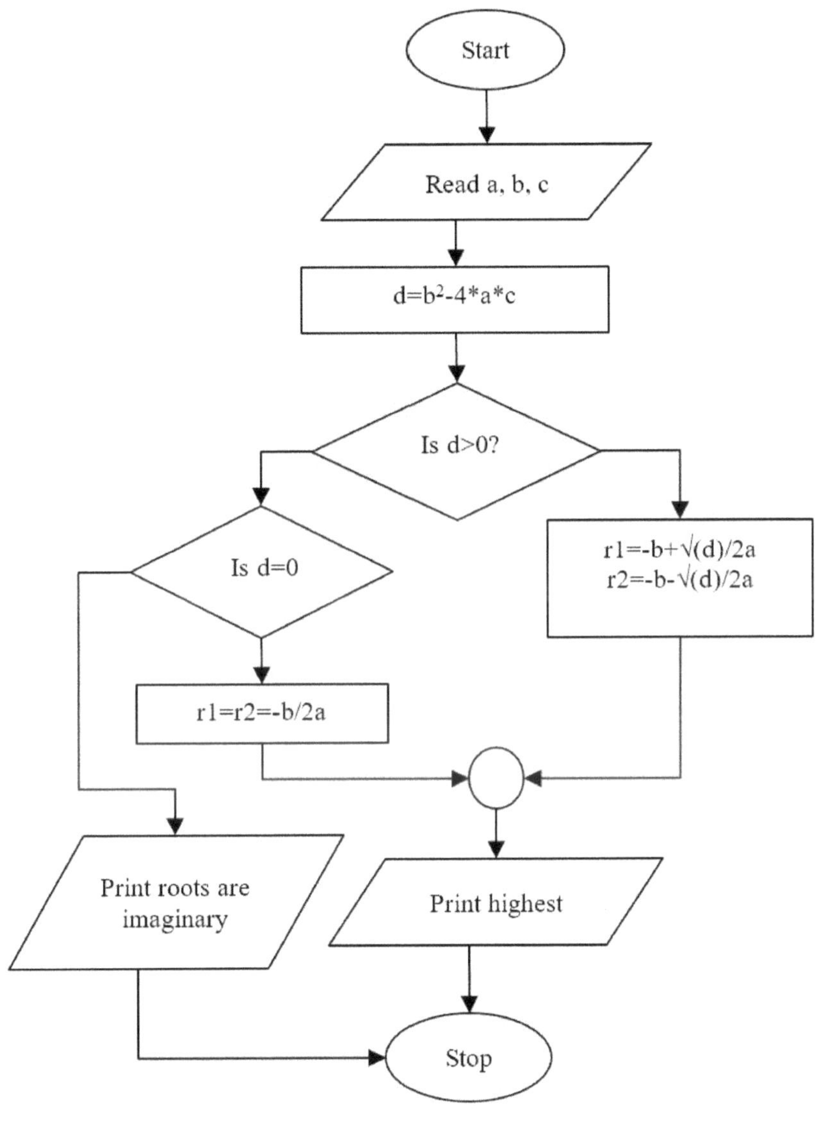

Program Development Steps

A Computer can neither think nor make any judgment of its own. So, it should be told exactly what to do, in a step-by-step fashion. The steps involved in a program development are:

1. *Problem Specification:* This step involves analysing the inputs provided, questions asked and output specifications of the problem.

2. *Outlining the Solution:* When once the problem is clear, a solution method for solving the problem has to be found, a path from what has been given to what is requires. There may be several methods to have a solution. The choice is made based on time-consumed and how far it is error-free.

3. *Selecting and representing Algorithm:* The solution method is described step-by-step here. The step-by-step procedure of the solution is an algorithm. So, an algorithm for the solution method is developed.

4. *The algorithm is programmed:* The algorithm prepared above has to be converted into a program using any of the programming languages. The choice of programming language is made based on the nature of problem and availability of programming languages.

5. *Removing errors:* A mistake in a program is known as error. Process of deleting and removing errors is called debugging. Errors are of 3 types.

   - *Syntax errors:* The grammatical rules of a programming language are called syntax. Errors occurred when these rules are not followed are known as syntax errors. These errors are found at the time of compiling and time errors. Error message is displayed by the compiler while executing the program.

Example: 1. Dividing a number by 0.

                        2. Square root of a negative number.

                        3. Logarithm of a negative number.

6. Testing and validation: Importance of testing is finding the errors and assurance of software quality. Testing is performed in two ways. They are:

   - Black Box Testing: The functionalities involved in the program are tested here.
     Example: calculations, input testing, error handling etc.
   - White Box Testing: This testing mainly concentrates on the control structure of the program.
     Example: path testing, condition testing etc.

7. Documentation and Maintenance: Documentation is the information that explains the usage as well as functionality of the software.

   - Operational Documentation: It provides the information regarding the input and output formats, operating instructions, different kinds of user interaction with the program and limitations if
   - Technical Documentation: It provides the technical details including the design aspects and brief explanation of the procedures involved, hardware to be operated.

Introduction to C

The programming language C was developed in 1972 by Dennis Ritchie at AT & T Bell Laboratories, USA. This was derived from a language called B, which was developed by Ken Thompson in 1970. The language B was derived from an existing language

BCPL (Basic Combined Programming Language) which was developed by Martin Richards in 1967.

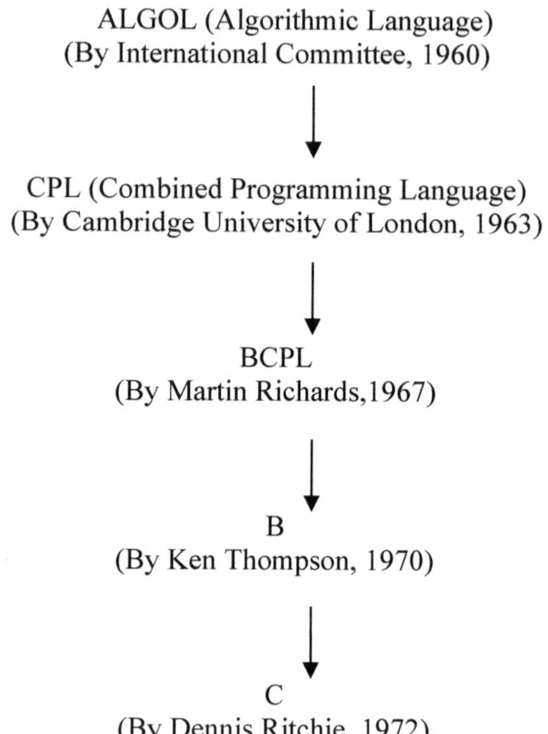

Characteristics of C

- 'C' is a structured programming high level language i.e., a C program can be divided into multiple blocks where each block represents a function.
- 'C' language is suitable for developing both application software as well as system software.
- It has wide variety of derived datatypes like arrays, structures, pointers and unions apart from fundamental datatypes like integers, floating point numbers and characters. This makes the language simple and small.
- 'C' is highly portable language. I.e., programs written in one machine can be easily run on some other machine without any modifications.

- Fast execution of programs when compared to other languages.
- 'C' provides a rich set of built-in functions and also has the ability to extend itself by defining own functions.
- 'C' supports all types of applications such as engineering, medical, scientific, marketing etc.

Structure of a 'C' Program

A 'C' Program contains the following sections:
- Documentation Section
- Link Section
- Definition Section
- Global Declaration Section
- main() function Section
- Sub program Section

Documentation Section: It consists of a set of comment lines which contain user interested details like name of author, program and any other details which makes the program more easy to understand.

Comment lines should be enclosed within /* and */ and can appear anywhere in the program. These comment lines are omitted by the compiler at the time of compilation.

Example:

```
/* program 1 */
/* QIS college */
```

Link Section: We know that 'C' has a rich set of built-in functions and they can be used to write any complex program. These standard functions are kept in various system libraries such as stdio.h (standard input-output header file), math.h (mathematical functions header file), ctype.h (character testing and conversion functions header file), string.h (string manipulations header file), conio.h (configuration input-output header file) etc.

If we want to use the functions of these libraries, we have to provide instructions to the compiler to link the functions from the corresponding system library. This can be achieved through link section of the 'C' program structure by using #include directive. Example:

```
#include<stdio.h>
#include<math.h>
```

Definition Section: Some problems require constant values to solve the problem. For Example: formula to find area of the circle is a= $\prod r^2$. Where $\prod$ is a constant whose value is 3.14. Such symbolic constants can be defined in definition section using #define directive.

Example:
```
#define pi 3.14
```

Global Declaration Section: There may be some variables that are used in more than one function. Such variables are called global variables and are declared in global declaration section i.e., outside of all the functions.

main( ) function Section: main( ) indicates starting of the program. Every 'C' program must have one main( ) function section. This section contains two parts.
   a) Declaration Section
   b) Executable Section

Declaration part declares all the variables used in the executable part and the entire code for the program is written in the executable part.

These two parts must appear between the opening and closing braces. The program execution begins at the opening brace and ends at the closing brace. All the statements in declaration part and executable part end with a semicolon (;).

Syntax:
```
                        main( )
                        {
                        // declaration part;
                          // executable part;
                        }
```

Subprogram Section: This section consists of one or more functions which are defined by the user. These functions can be called from main( ) function or any other user-defined function. User-defined functions are placed immediately after the main( ) function and they may appear in any order.

Note: All sections except the main( ) function section may be absent whey they are not required.

'C' Character Set:

The characters supported by 'C' language are:

a) Letters: a to z, A to Z
b) Digits: 0 to 9
c) Special Characters: , . ; : ? ' " ! ? / \ ~ -

                              % & | ^ + _ * < > ( ) [ ] { } # =

d) White spaces:

'C' Tokens

Smallest individual unit in a C program is known as a token. C has 6 types of tokens.

C Tokens

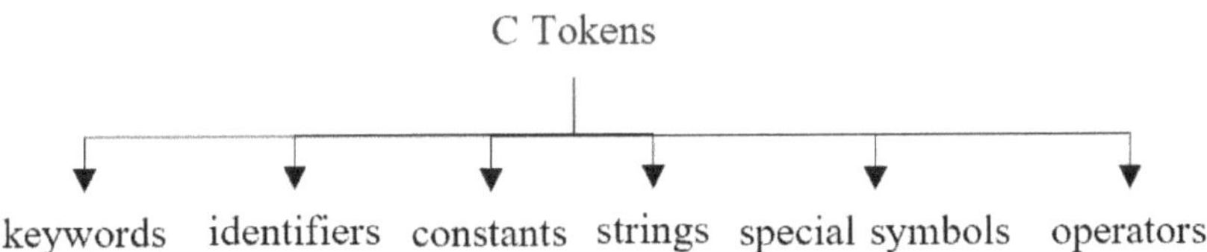

Keywords: Keywords are the English words which have fixed meaning which cannot be changed. Keywords should always be written in lowercase.

The keywords available in 'C' language are:

auto	double	int	struct
break	else	long	switch
case	enum	register	typedef
char	extern	return	union
const	float	short	unsigned

continue	for	signed	void
default	goto	sizeof	volatile
do	if	static	while

Identifier

Identifiers refer to the user-defined names such as names of variables, arrays, functions.

Constants

Constants refer to the fixed values that do not change during the execution of a program.

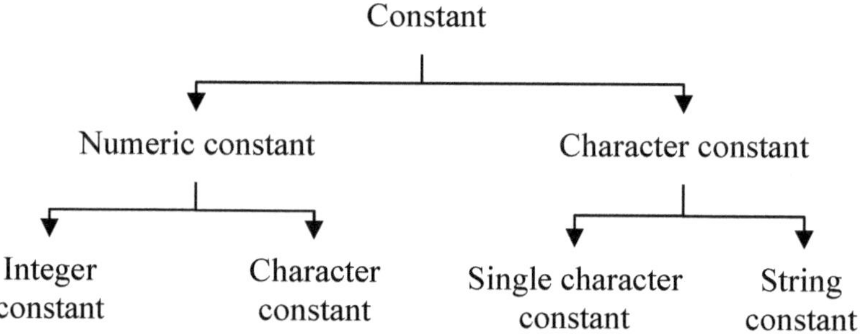

Integer Constants: An integer constant is a sequence of digits without any fractional parts.

There are three types of integer constants in C language. They are:

(i)   Decimal integer constants: It consists of set of digits 0 to 9, preceded by an optional sign + or -.
Example:

     +125, 0, -525, 68 etc.

(ii)   Octal integer constants: It consists of a set of digits 0 to 7, preceded by 0.
Example:

     0, 031, 0642, 0426 etc.

(iii)   Hexadecimal constants: It consists of a sequence of digits 0 to 9, A to F preceded by 0X. The letters A to F represents the numbers 10 to 15.

Example:

0X5, 0XF, OXABC etc.

Real Constants: Integer constants are not suitable to represent continuously varying quantities such as distances, heights, temperatures etc. These quantities can be represented by numbers containing fractional part. Such constants are known as real(or floating point) constants.
Example:
.7, -0.63, 7.5, 8.40, -0.0089 etc.
A real number may also be expressed in exponential notation.
Syntax:
```
mantissa e exponent
```
Example:
0.56e3, 10e-3, 3.5E3, -2.5E-2 etc.
Single Character Constants: A single character constant contains a single character enclosed within a pair of single quotation marks.

Example:
'5', 'x', ';', ' ' etc.
Every character value has an equivalent integer value known as ASCII value. ASCII stands for American Standard Code for Information Interchange.

String Constants: A string constant is a sequence of characters enclosed within a pair of double quotation marks.

Example:
"abcd", "2006", "A+B", "5+8" etc.

Symbolic Constants:
A symbolic Constant is a name that substitutes for a sequence of characters. The characters may represent a numeric constant, a character constant or a string constant.

```
# define name text
```

Where name represents a symbolic name, typically written in uppercase letters, and text represents the sequence of characters associated with the symbolic name. Note that text does not end with a semicolon.

```
# define TAXRATE 0.25
# define PI      3.1415
# define TRUE    1
# define FALSE   0
# define FRIEND  "rama"
```

Notice that the symbolic names are written in uppercase, to distinguish them from ordinary C identifiers.

Variables

A variable is one which is used to store a datavalue. A variable may take different values at different times during program execution. The following rules have to be followed while declaring a variable.

i)   It consists of letters, digits, underscore character(_).
ii) Must begin with a letter or an underscore.
iii) Maximum distinguishable length should be 8 characters.
iv) It should not be a keyword.
v)   White spaces are not allowed.

Example: x, a1, value, a_b, sum etc

Basic Datatypes and Sizes

Data given to the system may be of different types like integers, real numbers, letters, words etc. Each and every data has to be represented with the appropriate datatype. Datatypes are classified into four:

i)   Primary datatype
ii) Derived datatype
iii) User-defined datatype
iv) Empty dataset.

o   *Primary datatypes:* There are three fundamental datatypes in C. They are:

(a) integer
(b) floating point
(c) character

(a) **Integer:** Integers are the whole numbers in the range – 32768 to +32767 including 0. An integer can be represented with the keyword *int.* It is stored in 16 bits as its storage location. An integer can be stored as short int, int, long int both in signed and unsigned forms depending upon the value stored.

Type	Size	Range
int or signed int	2 bytes	-32768 to +32767
unsigned int	2 bytes	0 to 65535
short int or signed short int	1 byte	-128 to +127
unsigned short int	1 byte	0 to 255
long int or signed long int	4 byte	-2147483648to+2147483647
unsigned long int	4 bytes	0 to 4294967295

(b) **Floating point**: Real numbers are represented using the datatype *float.* Floating point numbers are stored in 32 bits with 6 digits of precision. To improve the accuracy, we go for the datatype double, which is an extension of floating point datatype. A double datatype number uses 64 bits with a precision of 14 digits

Type	Size	Range
float	4 bytes	3.4e-38 to 3.4e+38
double	8 bytes	1.7e-308 to 1.7e+308
long double	10 bytes	3.4e-4932 to 1.1e+4932

(c) **character**: Characters are defined by the datatype *char.* These are usually stored in 8 bits of internal storage.

Type	Size	Range
signed char	1 byte	-128 to +127

unsigned char	1 byte	0 to 255

- o   *User-defined datatypes: typedef* is a user-defined datatype used to define an identifier that would represent an existing datatype.

```
Syntax: typedef datatype identifier;
Example:   typedef int marks;
                  marks s1,s2;
```

Another user-defined datatype available is enumerated datatype *enum*.

Syntax:

```
        enum identifier {  value1, value2,  ......,
value n};
```

Example:
```
enum day { Monday, Tuesday, Wednesday
........, Sunday };
                  enum day week_st,week_end;
```

- o   *Derived datatype:* Derived datatypes are the datatypes such as arrays, functions, structures, pointers.

- o   *Empty dataset: void* is the keyword used to specify empty dataset. The void type has no values. This is usually used to specify the type of functions.

A Program to enter initial and name and display the same.

```
/* program 1*/
#include<stdio.h>
#include<conio.h>
void main( )
{
char ch,name[10];
puts("enter your initial");
ch=getchar( );
puts("enter your name");
```

```c
gets(name);
puts("the name you have entered is ");
putchar(ch);
puts(name);
getch( );
}
```

A Program to convert lower case letter to its equivalent upper case.

```c
        /* program 2*/
#include<stdio.h>
#include<conio.h>
void main( )
{
char ch;
puts("enter any character in  lower case");
ch=getchar( );
ch=ch-32;
puts("the  equivalent  upper  case  character
is");
putchar(ch);
getch( );
}
```

Operators

An operator is a symbol that tells the compiler to perform certain mathematical or logical manipulation. The value on which an operation is performed is called operand.

'C' operators can be classified into different categories. They are:

Arithmetic operators: These are the operators which perform mathematical manipulations. The available arithmetic operators are:

$$+ \quad \rightarrow \text{ addition or unary plus}$$

- → subtraction or unary minus
* → multiplication
/ → division
% → modulo division

Example:

a+b, 25%5, x-y*z, 52/2 etc.

Relational operators: These are the operators used to compare 2 values or expressions. The available relational operators are:

< → less than
<= → less than or equal to
> → greater than
>= → greater than or equal to
== → equal to
!= → not equal to

Example:

x<y, 50>=25, (35+70)==(75+30), a!=b etc.

Logical operators: These are the operators used to combine two or more expressions. The available relational operators are:

&& → logical AND
|| → logical OR
! → logical NOT

Example:

n>0&&n<=100, x==5!!x==10, !(x<y) etc.

Assignment operators: These are the operators used to assign a value or result of an expression to a variable. The assignment operator available is '='. This can be used with any of the arithmetic operators +,-,*,/,% like +=,-=,*=,/=,%=.
Example:

a+=5 means a=a+5
b-=10 means b=b-10
c*=2 means c=c*2
d/=6 means d=d/6
e%=10 means e=e%10

Increment and decrement operators: These are the two unary operators which operate on a single operand. These operators can be used in two forms: prefix or postfix. When prefix++ (or--) is used in an expression, the variable is incremented (or decremented) first and then the expression is evaluated with the new value of the variable. When postfix ++ (or --) is used, the expression is evaluated first and then the value of variable is incremented (or decremented).

Example:

    for prefix:

            a=5;
                b=++a;

Example:

    for postfix:

                a=5;
                b=a++;

Conditional operator: This is a ternary operator which takes the form:

            exp 1? exp 2: exp 3;

Here, the exp1 is evaluated first. If it is true, then exp2 becomes the value of the expression. If exp1 is false, then exp 3 becomes the value of the expression.

Example:

        x=5;
        y=8;
        z=(x>y)?x:y;

Bitwise operators: These operators are used for manipulation of data at bit level.

The bitwise operators are

                        & → bitwise AND
                        | → bitwise OR
                        ^   → bitwise EX- OR
                        << → shift left
                        >> → shift right

Example: x=5

y=6

x&y: 0101	x|y: 0101	x^y: 0101
0110	0110	0110
0100	0111	0011

Let a=01001011

a<<3 = 01011000

a>>4 = 00001001

Precedence of Operators

While executing an arithmetic statement, which has two or more operators, we may have some problems about how exactly does it get executed

For example does the expression

a+b*c correspond to (a+b) * c or a + (b*c)

The order of priority in which the operations are performed in an expression is called precedence.

An arithmetic expression without parenthesis will be evaluated from left to right. using the rules of precedence of operators

High priority   *   /   %

Low priority   +   -

The basic evaluation procedure includes two passes from left to right through the expression. During the first pass the high priority operators (if any) are applied as they are encountered. During the second pass the low priority operators (if any) are applied as they are encountered.

```
float    a,b,c,x,y,z;
a=9;
b=12;
c=3;
x = a-b / 3+c * 2 - 1;
```

```c
y = a-b / (3+c) * (2-1);
z = a-(b/ (3+c) * 2) -1;
printf ("x = %f\n",x);
printf("y = %f\n",y);
printf("z = %f\n",z);
```

....

Whenever parenthesis are used the expressions within parenthesis assume highest priority. If two or more sets of parenthesis appear one after the another as 9-12/(3+3)*(2-1). The expression contained in the left most set is evaluated first and the right most in the last.

$$9-12/(3+3)*(2-1)$$
$$9-12/6*(2-1)$$
$$9-12/6*1$$
$$9-2*1$$
$$9-2$$
$$7.$$

Parenthesis may be nested, and in such cases, evaluation of the expression will proceed outward from the innermost set of parenthesis.

9-(12/(3+3)*2)-1
9-(12/6*2)-1
9-(2*2)-1
9-4-1
  4.

9-((12/3)+3*2)-1
9-(4+3*2)-1
9-(4+6)-1
9-10-1
-2.

Type Conversions

automatically converts lower type to higher type before the operation performs and ultimately the result is of the higher type. This is known as *implicit conversion*.

Example:

```c
int a, x;
float b;
double c;
```

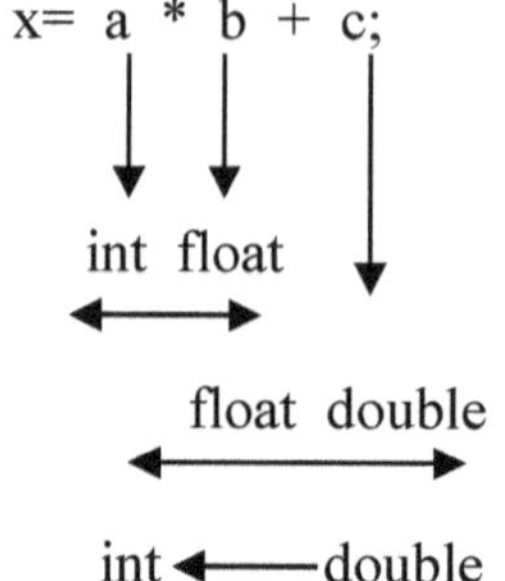

We can also perform type conversion explicitly by using a unary operator called cast operator, in the following way:

(type name) expression.

where type name is any of the C datatypes and expression may be a constant, variable or expression.

Example:

```
a=(int)8.6=8
x=(float)7=7.0
y=(int)6.5/(int)2.3=6/2=3
b=(int)(a+b)
```

Expressions: An expression is a combination of variables, constants and operators.

Example:

```
a*b+c, x+y-z,5*a+b+6*c,(a+b)*(x+y).
```

Evaluation of Expressions:

An expression can be evaluated based on the precedence of operators. After the expression is evaluated, then the value of the expression is assigned to the variable.

Example:

```
x=5*6-4=26
A=3+2*6=15
z=3%2+1=2
```

Example:

progam

```
void main()
{
int a,b,c,x,y,z,w;
```

```
a=2;
b=3;
c=4;
x=a+b-c+a;
y=a-b+c%a;
z=a*b-(c+a);
w=a-(10/(1+c)*2)-1;
printf("%d%d%d%d%d",x,y,z,w);
getch();
}
```

Escape sequences:

Constant	meaning
\a	audible alert
\b	backspace
\f	form feed
\n	new line
\t	horizontal tab
\v	vertical tab
\'	generate single quote
\"	generatedouble quote
\?	Generate question mark
\\	generate backslash
\0	null character

Input/Output Statements

Input functions: These functions are used to enter data into the system.

(i) *getchar( ):* This function takes a single character as input and stores it in the given variable name.

Syntax:
```
variable name=getchar( );
```
Example:
```
x=getchar( );
```
It assigns the value to the variable after the Enter key is pressed.

(ii)   *getche( ):* This function takes a single character from the keyboard and assigns it to the given variable name without waiting for the Enter key to be pressed.

Syntax:
```
variable name=getche( );
```
Example:
```
x=getche( );
```

(iii)   *getch( ):* This function takes a single character from the keyboard.

Syntax:
```
getch( );
```

(iv)   *gets( ):* This function takes a group of characters at a time from the keyboard and stores in the given variable name.

Syntax:
```
gets(variable name);
```
Example:
```
gets(name);
```

(v)   *scanf( ):* It is a standard 'C' library function. This function is used to enter input data. Input data may be numerical values, single characters, strings. These input values are assigned to corresponding variables.

Syntax:
```
scanf("control            strings",
&variable         1,&variable2,......,
&variable n);
```
Example:
```
scanf("%d%c%f", &i, &x, &p);
```
In the above example, i accepts integer type value, x accepts single character, p accepts floating-point value

Output functions:

These functions are used to display the data from the system.

(i)   *putchar( ):* This function is used to display a single character stored in the given variable name.

Syntax:
```
putchar(variable name);
```
Example:
```
char x='a';
putchar(a);
```

(ii)   *puts( ):* This function is used to display a group of characters stored in a variable name.

Syntax:
```
puts(variable name);
```
Example:
```
char name[ ]="qis";
puts(name);
```
It is also used to display a given matter on the output screen.

Example:
```
puts("enter your name");
```

(iii)   *printf( ):* This is a standard 'C' library function which is used to display data items. It can be used to print captions, numerical values, characters, strings.

Syntax:
```
printf("control strings",variable1,
variable2,……..,variable n);
```
Example:
```
printf("%d%c%f",x,i,p);
```

Control strings indicates how many values are to be printed and what are the types of the values. Variable1, variable2, ……..variable n are the variables whose values are to be printed according to the specification of control string. The variables should match in number, order and type with the control string.

%c	single character
%d	decimal integer
%e	floating point value
%f	floating point value
%s	string
%x	Hexa decimal
%o	Octal

Control Statements

Control statements are classified into 4 types
1. Sequence Control statements
2. Selection Control statements (if& switch)
3. Iterative [Loop] Control statements (for &While)
4. Jump Control Statements

1. Sequence Control statements: all statements will be executed in sequential manner ie line by line manner

```
1---------------
2---------------
3---------------
4--------------
        .

        .

n--------------
```

2.Selection Control statements: Based on the decision it will executes the statements these are two types IF, SWITCH

If **Statement**

Generally, the control in a program will be in sequential order. i.e., it executes the statements in top-down approach.

'*if*' is used to control the sequence of statements based on a given condition. 'if' can be used in the following forms.

(i)   ***Simple if:*** This *'if'* statement contains true part. i.e., whenever the condition is true, then only the statement or statements will get executed.

Syntax:
```
if(condition)
{
statement block;
}
statement-x;
```

Flowchart:

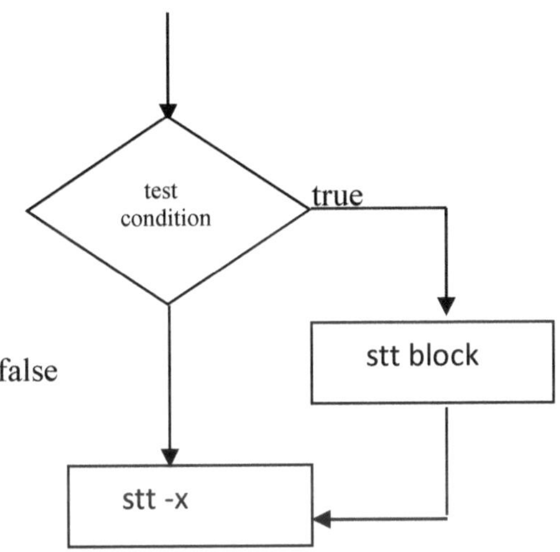

Example:
```
1.if(a>b)
printf("a is big");

2. if(x==10)
{
  x=x+10;
printf("%d",x);
}
```

(ii)   ***if-else:*** if-else structure contains two parts. One is true part and other is the false part but only one of these two parts is executed based on the condition tested.

Syntax:

```
if(test condition)
{
statement block-1;
}
else
{
statement block-2;
}
statement-x;
```

Flowchart:

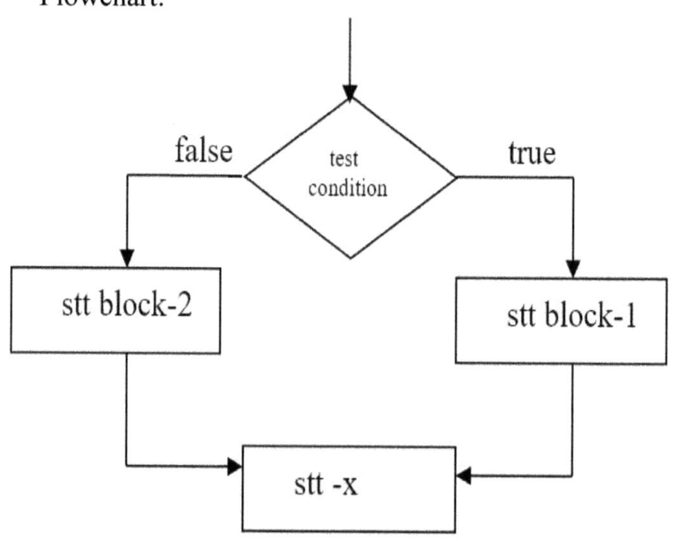

Example:

```
if(a>b)
printf("a is big");
else
printf(" b is big");
```

In the above syntax, statement block 1 will be executed if the condition becomes true. Otherwise statement block 2 will be executed. Statement –x will be executed in both the cases.

(iii) *Nested if-else:* Whenever a series of decisions are to be made, more than one if-else statements are to be used within one another. This is known as nested if-else.

Syntax:

```
if(test condition1)
{
if(test condtion 2)
{
statement block-1;
}
else
{
statement block 2;
}
}
else
{
statement block 3;
}
statement-x;
```

Flowchart:

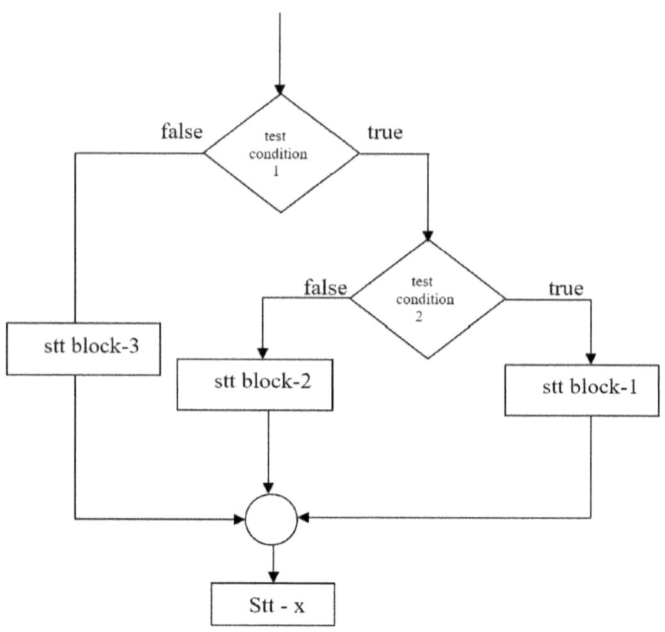

Example:

```
if(a>b)
{
if(a>c)
printf("a is big");
else
printf("c is big");
}
else if(b>c)
{
printf("b is big");
}
else
printf("c is big");
```

(iii)   *else-if* **ladder:** Whenever a condition has to be tested based on the falsity of the above condition, else-if ladder can be used.

Syntax:

```
if(test condition 1)
{
statement block-1;
}
else if(test condition 2)
{
statement block-2;
}
else if(test condition 3)
{
statement block-3;
}
else
{
default statement
}
statement-x;
```

Flowchart:

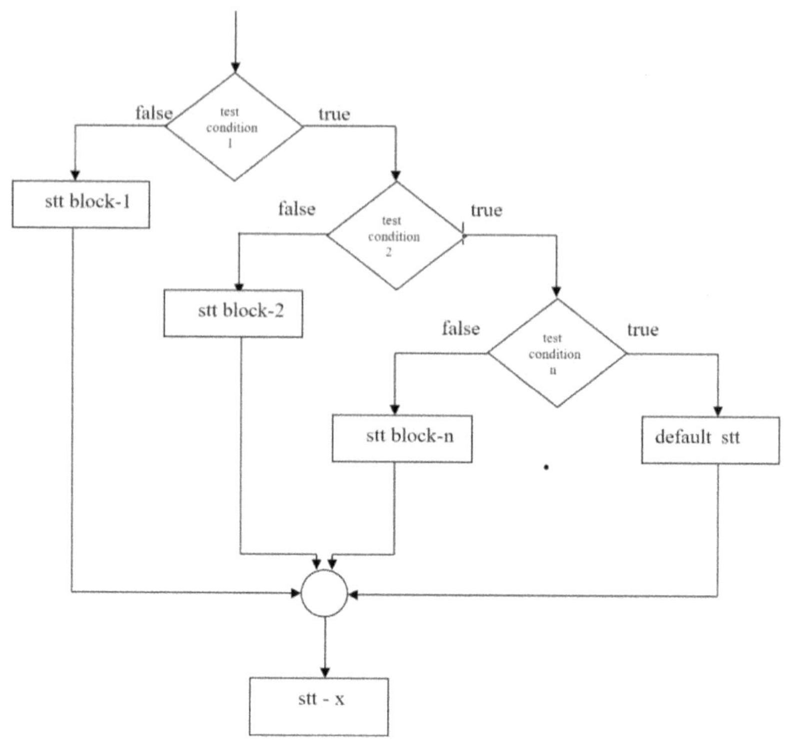

Example:
```
if(a>b&&a>c&&a>d)
printf("a is big");
else f(b>c&&b>d)
printf("b is big");
else if(c>d)
printf("c is big");
else
printf("d is big");
```

A Program to find whether a year is leap year or not using if-else.

```
#include<stdio.h>
#include<conio.h>
void main( )
{

    int year;
```

```c
                    printf("enter any year\n");
                    scanf("%d",&year);
                    if(year%4==0&&year%100==0||y
                    ear%400==0)
                    printf("%d is a leap
                    year",year);
                    else
                    printf("%d is not a leap
                    year",year);
                    getch( );
              }
```

A Program to find roots of a quadratic equation.

```c
#include<stdio.h>
#include<conio.h>
void main( )
{
int a,b,c,d;
float r1,r2;
clrscr( );
printf("enter a,b,c");
scanf("%d%d%d",&a,&b,&c);
d=b*b-4*a*c;
if(d>0)
{
   r1=((-b+sqrt(d))/(2*a));
   r2=((-b-sqrt(d))/(2*a));
   printf("roots are %f,%f",r1,r2);
}
        else if (d==0)
        {
            r1=r2=(-b/(2*a));
            printf("roots are %f,%f",r1,r2);
        }
        else
        {
```

```c
      printf("roots are imaginary");
      }
    getch( );  }
```

A Program to print the grade of a student based on the below conditions:

```
m>35,p>35,c>36→ pass
avg>=80→distinction
60<=avg<80→1st class
50<=avg<60→2nd class
avg<0→3rd class
```

```c
void main( )
{
 int m,p,c;
 float avg;
 printf("enter marks");
 scanf("%d%d%d",&m,&p,&c);
 avg=(m+p+c)/3;
 if(m>35&&p>35&&c>35)
     {
     if(avg>=80)
     printf("distinction");
     else if(avg>=60&&avg<80)
     printf("first class");
     else if(avg>=50&&avg<60)
     printf("second class");
     else
     printf("third class")
    }
    else
         {
              printf("fail");
         }
    getch( );
}
```

A Program to generate electricity bill.

```c
void main( )
{
float charge,units;
printf("enter number of units");
scanf("%f",&units);
if(units>0&&units<=200)
      {
      charge=units*1.0;
      printf("charge=%f",charge);
      }
else  if(units>200&&units<=400)
      {
      charge=(units-200)*1.50+200*1.0;
 printf("charge=%f",charge);
      }
else  if(units>400&&units<=800)
      {
charge=(units-
800)*5.0+400*2.0+200*1.5+200*1.0;
printf("charge=%f",charge);
      }
      getch( );
}
```

***Switch* STATEMENT:**

It is a selection statement where we can select one alternative from different alternatives. i.e., we can make one group of statements to execute among many options.

Syntax:

```c
switch(expression)
{
case label 1: stts;
break;
case label 2:  stts;
break;
```

```
        :
        :
        :
case label n: stts;
break;
default:stts;
break;
}
stt-x;
```

Flowchart:

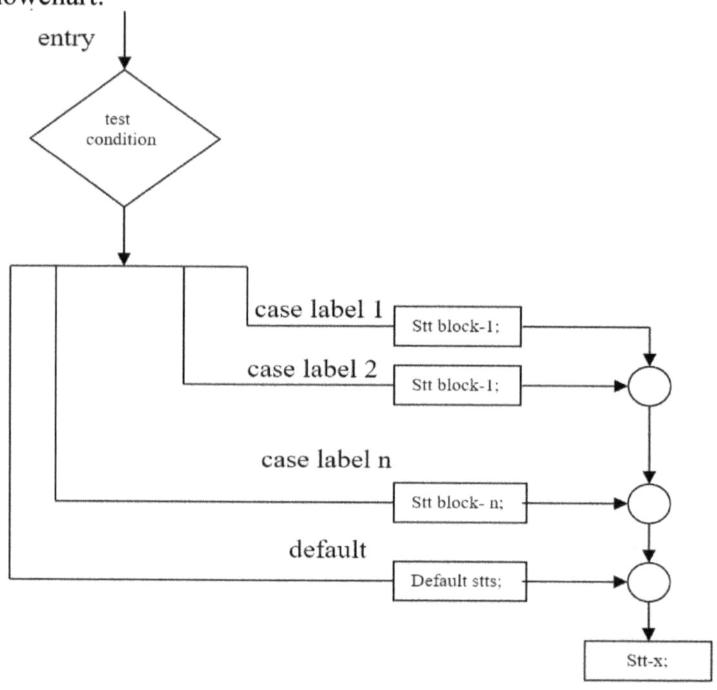

The expression may be an integer expression or characters.

A Program to perform corresponding arithmetic operation based on the operator.

```c
#include<stdio.h>
#include<conio.h>
void main()
{
     int a,b,c;
```

```c
char ch;
clrscr();
printf("Enter the value of a\t\n");
scanf("%d",&a);
printf("Enter the value of b \t \n");
scanf("%d",&b);
printf("***********");
printf("\n MENU \n");
printf("***********");
printf("\n 1.Addition \n");
printf("\n 2.Subtraction \n");
printf("\n 3.Multiplication \n");
printf("\n 4.Division \n");
while(ch!='n')
    {
       printf("\n Enter u r choice\t\n");
        scanf("%c",&ch);
        switch(ch)
        {
              case '+':
              c=a+b;
              printf("The sum is: %d",c);
              break
              case '-':
              c=a-b;
              printf("The difference is:
              %d",c);
              break;
              case '*':
              c=a*b;
              printf("The Product is: %d",c);
              break;
              case '/':
              c=a/b;
              printf("The quotient is: %d",c);
                    break;
                                            }
                }
                  getch( );
}
```

A Program to display the corresponding weekday according to the number given.

```c
void main( )
{
  int n;
  printf("enter any number");
  scanf("%d",&n);
  switch(n)
{
case 1: printf("Monday");
break;
case 2: printf("Tuesday");
break;
case 3: printf("Wednesday");
break;
case 4: printf("Thursday");
break;
case 5: printf("Friday");
break;
case 6: printf("Saturday");
break;
case 7: printf("Sunday");
break;
default:       printf("no       corresponding
weekday");
break;
}
      getch( );
      }
```

3.Iterative [Loop] Control statements (for & While)

Loops:
Executing a set of statements repeatedly some number of times or until some condition, is called looping.

Looping Statements: In looping, a sequence of statements are executed until some conditions for termination of the loop are satisfied. A program loop therefore consists of two Segments.

One has known as the body of the loop and the other known as the control statements. The control stmt tests certain conditions and then directs the repeated execution of the statements. contained in the body of the loop.

C language provides 3 loop structures
1. The while statement
2. Do-While statement
3. For statement

while loop:

while is an entry controlled loop. Here, first the condition is evaluated and if the condition is true then the statement block will be executed as many times until the condition becomes false.

Syntax:

```
while(test condition)
{
statement block;
}
statement-x;
```

Flowchart:

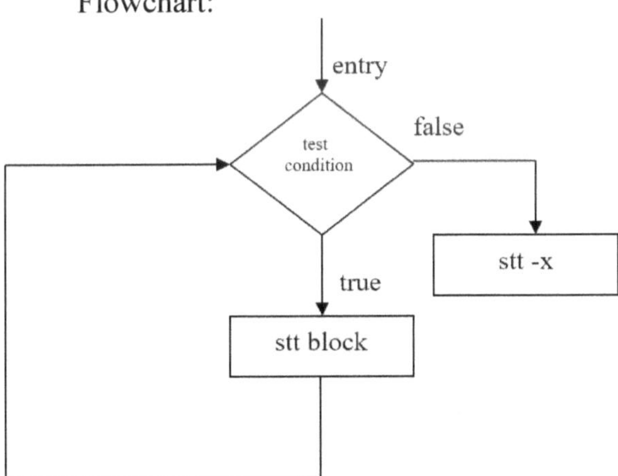

A Program to print first n natural numbers using while loop.

```
void main( )
```

```
{
int i,n;
printf("enter n");
scanf("%d",&n);
i=1;
while(i<=n)
{
printf("%d\n",i);
i++;
      }
      getch( );
       }
```

A Program to print numbers from n to 1 using while loop.

```
void main( )
{
int i,n;
printf("enter n");
scanf("%d",&n);
while(n>=1)
{
printf("%d\n",n);
n--;
      }
      getch( );
    }
```

A Program to print even numbers using while loop.

```
void main( )
{
int i,n;
printf("enter n");
scanf("%d",&n);
i=2;
while(i<=n)
{
printf("%d\n",i);
i=i+2;
      }
          getch( );
      }
```

A Program to print sum of first n natural numbers using while loop.

```
void main()
{
int i=1,n,sum=0;
printf("enter n");
scanf("%d",&n);
while(i<=n)
{
sum=sum+i;
i++;
        }
printf("%d\n",sum);
getch( );
      }
```

A Program to find sum of individual digits of a given number using while loop.

```
#include<stdio.h>
#include<conio.h>
void main( )
{
  int n,s=0,r;
clrscr( );
 printf("enter any number");
 scanf("%d",&n);
 while(n>0)
 {
  r=n%10;
  s=s+r;
  n/=10;
   }
 printf("sum=%d",s);
 getch( );  }
```

A Program to find reverse of a given number using while loop.

```
#include<stdio.h>
```

```c
#include<conio.h>
void main( )
{
 int n,rev=0,r;
clrscr( );
 printf("enter any number");
 scanf("%d",&n);
 while(n>0)
 {
  r=n%10;
  rev=rev*10+r;
  n/=10;
 }
 printf("reverse=%d",rev);
getch( );
}
```

A Program to check whether a number is Armstrong or not.

```c
#include<stdio.h>
#include<conio.h>
void main( )
     {
int r,n,sum=0,tn;
printf("enter any number\n");
scanf(%d",&n);
while(n>0)
{
r=n%10;
sum =sum+r*r*r;
n/=10;
       }
if(tn==sum)
printf("%d is armstrong",sum);
else
printf("%d is not Armstrong",sum)
             getch( );
             }
```

do-while:

This is an exit control loop structure. Here the statement block is executed first and then the condition is tested. If the condition is true, the statement block is executed once again. This process continues until the condition becomes false. When once the condition is false, the control will come out of the loop. i.e., all the statements that are enclos3ed between do-while are executed at least once.

Syntax:

```
do
{
statement   block;
increment/decrement;
}while(condition);
```

Flowchart:

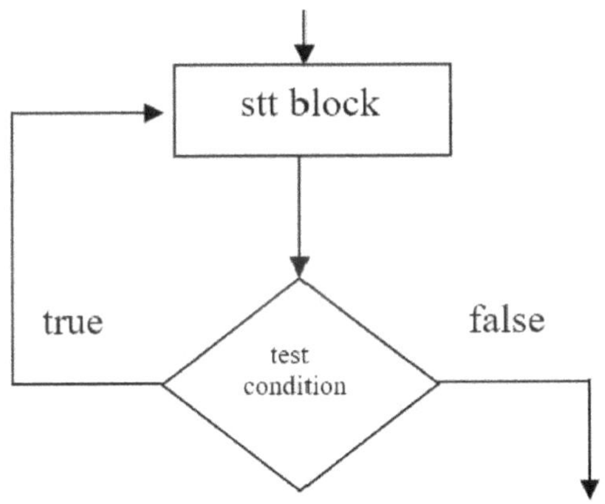

Example:

```
int  i=1;
do
{
printf("%d",i);
i++;
}
    while(i>1);
```

A Program to print average of n numbers using do-while loop.

```c
#include<stdio.h>
#include<conio.h>
void main( )
{
int i=1,n,m;
float sum=0,avg;
clrscr( );
printf("enter n value");
scanf("%d",&n);
printf("enter values\n");
do
{
scanf("%d",&m);
sum=sum+m;
i++;
   }
while(i<=n);
avg=sum/n;
printf("average=%f",avg);
getch( );
}
```

A Program to count the number of individual digits of a given number.

```c
#include<stdio.h>
#include<conio.h>
void main( )
{
int n,r,c=0;
clrscr( );
printf("enter any number");
scanf("%d",&n);
do{
r=n%10;
c++;
n/=10;
}
while(n>0);
printf("number of individual digits=%d",c);
}
```

for

for is an entry control loop statement which executes the statements to a specified number of times. It contains three parts.

Syntax:

```
        for(initialization; test
condition; increment/decrement)
          {
            statement block;
          }
```

Initialization of the loop control variable is done first and then the condition is tested. If the condition is true, then the statement block will be executed and then incrementation or decrementation is done as specified for the next iteration. The execution of the statement block continues until the condition is true and when once the condition becomes false, the control will come out from the loop.

A Program to calculate sum of squares of first n natural numbers.

```c
#include<stdio.h>
#include<conio.h>
void main()
{
int i,n,sum=0;
clrscr( );
printf("enter n value");
scanf("%d",&n);

for(i=1;i<=n;i++)
   {
sum=sum+i*i;
   }
printf("sum=%d",sum);
}
```

A Program to print multiplication table of a number.

```c
#include<stdio.h>
#include<conio.h>
 void main( )
{
int i,n,r;
clrscr( );
printf("enter n value");
scanf("%d",&n);
 for(i=1;i<=10;i++)
{
r=n*i;
printf("%d*%d=%d",n,i,r);
}
getch( );}
```

A Program to find factorial without using recursion.

```c
#include<stdio.h>
#include<conio.h>
void main( )
{
int i,n,fact=1;
clrscr( );
printf("enter any number\n");
scanf("%d",&n);
for(i=1;i<=n;i++)
{
    fact=fact*i;
}
 printf("factorial of %d is %d",n,fact);
 getch( );
}
```

<u>Nested for:</u> one for loop existing in another for loop is known as nesting of for loops. Whenever there are two loops within one another, the inner loop execution takes place first and then the control goes to outer loop.

Example: `for(i=1;i<=5;i++)`
        `{`

```c
for(j=1;j<=5;j++)
{
printf("%d ",i);
}
printf("\n");
```

A Program to print the sequence

```
                              1
                         1        2
                    1         2         3
```

```c
#include<stdio.h>
#include<conio.h>
void main( )
{
int i,j,n;
printf("enter number of rows\n");
scanf("%d",&n);
for(i=1;i<=n;i++)
for(j=1;j<=i;j++)
printf("%d\t",j);
printf("\n");
getch( );
}
```

A Program to print the sequence

```
              1
         2         3
     4         5         6
7         8         9         10
```

```c
#include<stdio.h>
#include<conio.h>
void main( )
{
int i,j,n,k,l=1;
clrscr( );
printf("enter number of rows");
scanf("%d",&n);
for(i=1;i<=n;i++)
   {
   for(j=1;j<=(n-i);j++)
   printf("   ");
```

```
    for(k=1;k<(2*i-1);k++)
    {
     if(k%2==0)
     printf(" ");
     else
     printf("%d\t",1++);
    }
}
getch( );
}
```

A Program to print prime numbers between 1 and n.

```
void main( )
{
int i,j,n,;
clrscr( );
printf("enter any number");
scanf("%d",&n);
for(i=1;i<=n;i++)
        {
     for(j=2;j<i;j++)
     {
            if(i%j==0)
            count++;
             }
if(count==0)
printf("%d\t",i);
        }
getch( );
}
```

A Program to calculate the following sum

$$1+x^2/2! + x^4/4! +---- \text{ n terms.}$$

```
#include<stdio.h>
#include<conio.h>
#include<math.h>
void main( )
    {
        int i,n,fact,x;
```

```c
float sum=1;
clrscr( );
printf("Enter the Value\n");
scanf("%d",&n);
printf("Enter the value of x:\n");
 scanf("%d",&x);
 or(i=2;i<=2*(n-1);i+=2)
    {
         fact*=i*(i-1);
            sum+=pow(x,i)/(fact,i);
    }
         printf("Result= %f",sum);
         getch( );
 }
```

break:

It is generally used to come out from a loop or to exit from a switch. This statement can be used within for, while, do-while, switch.

Syntax:
```c
break;
```
Example:
```c
for(i=1;i<=110;i++)
{
if(i==5)
break;
printf("%d",i);
}
printf("out of loop");
```

continue:

This statement is used to skip a part of loop for the current iteration and continue with the next iteration. This can be used within while, do-while, for.

Syntax:
```c
continue;
```

Example:

```c
for(i=1;i<=110;i++)
{
if(i==5)
continue;
printf("%d",i);
}
printf("out of loop");
```

A Program to calculate square root of a positive number using continue statement.

```c
#include<stdio.h>
#include<conio.h>
void main( )
{
int i,x,s;
clrscr( );
printf("enter values\n");
for(i=1;i<=10;i++)
    {
        scanf("%d",&x);
            if(x<0)
    continue;
            s=sqrt(x);
            printf("square root of %d is
%d\n",x,s);
        }
        getch( );
}
```

exit( ):
This is used to stop the program execution and come out from the program whenever we like to.
Syntax: `exit(0);`
Example: prog:
```c
void main()
{
int i;
for(i=0;i<=10;i++)
{
```

```c
if(i==5)
exit(0);
printf("%d",x);
}
printf("out of loop");
}
```

go to:

This is used to change the normal program execution by transferring the control loop to some part of the program.

Syntax:
```c
go to label;
label:
statement block;
```

Label may be any identifier that is used to label the target statements to which the control will be transferred. The target statements must be labeled and the label must be followed by a colon. No two statements can have the same label.

Example:
```c
abc:
printf("enter value");
scanf("%d",&x);
if(x<0)
{
printf("u have entered a negative value");
go to abc;
}
sum=sum+x;
printf("%d",sum);
}
```

2. Functions and Storage Classes

Objective

1.   Learn how to declare and call functions
2.   Understanding various Operations in functions
3.   Provide knowledge of storage classes and pre-processor concepts

Introducing the fundamental concepts of functions and storage classes in programming unveils the dynamic layers of code organization and memory management. Functions, akin to modular building blocks, encapsulate specific tasks, fostering code reusability and maintainability. As the essential units of program execution, they facilitate a structured and modular approach to problem-solving. Concurrently, the exploration of storage classes delves into the nuanced management of memory and variable scope within a program. Understanding storage classes provides developers with the tools to control the lifetime and visibility of variables, optimizing memory usage and enhancing the overall efficiency of the code. Together, functions and storage classes form the backbone of structured programming, offering a powerful framework for creating robust and efficient software solution

Introduction to Functions

C function can be classified into two categories
1. Library functions.
2. User defined functions.

main( ) is an example of user defined function. printf, scanf, sqrt, cos, strcat belong to the category of library functions.

 Every program must have a main function to indicate where the program has to begin its execution. If a program was coded as a single function, the program may become too large and complex and as a result the task of debugging, testing and maintaining becomes difficult. If a program is divided into functional parts then each art may be independently coded and later combined into a single unit. These sub programs called functions are much easier to understand, debug and test.

If a program is divided into functional parts, then each part may be independently coded and later combined into a single unit.

A function is a self-contained block of code that performs a particular task.

```
type function_name (argument list)
    argument declaration;
    {
      local variable declarations;
    stmt1;
    stmt2;
    -

    -

    return (expression);
    }
```

All parts are not essential. Some may be absent. For example, the argument list and its associated argument declaration parts are optional.

The return statement is the mechanism for returning a value to the calling function. This is also an optional statement. Its absence indicates that no value is being returned to the calling function.

The argument list contains valid variable names separated by commas. The list must be surrounded by parenthesis. All argument variables must be declared for their types after the function header and before the opening brace of the function box.

A function may or may not send back any value to the calling function. If it does, it is done through the return statement. Function can return at most one value per call.

A function name can be called by simply using the function name in a statement.

Example
```
int mul(a,b)
int a,b;
{
      int m;
      m=a*b;
      return(m);
}
main( )
{
      int p;
      p=mul(10,5);       /* function call */
      printf("%d\n",p);
}
```

When the compiler encounters a function call, the control is transferred to the function mul(x,y). This function is then executed line by line and a value is returned when a return statement is encountered. This value is assigned to p.

Points to remember
1. A function may or may not return a value if it does, it can return only one value.
2. Functions return integer value by default.
3. When a function is supposed to return a non-integer value, its type must be explicitly specified in the function header. Such a function should be declared at the start of the calling function.

Definition: A functions is self-contained block or sub-program of one or more statements that perform a specific task.

a) Library functions are a predefined set of functions which are already defined for specific tasks and the definitions are enclosed in corresponding header files. These functions cannot be modified by men.

Example:
```
printf( ), scanf( ), getchar( ), sqrt( ), etc.,
```

b) User also has an opportunity to define his own functions. The functions defined by the user based on the users requirement are called user-defined functions. The names of the functions can also be of user interest. But, the rules for identifiers have to be followed in declaring the names of functions.

A user defined function can be modified according to the changing requirement.

In order to develop a user-defined function the following parts have to be developed.

1. Function declaration.
2. Function call
3. Function definition.

Function declaration (or) Function Prototype

Likewise a variable is declared before it is used in the program a user-defined function also has to be declared with an appropriate data type.

Syntax:
```
data type function name (parameters);
```

Here the data type indicated the type of value returned after the function is performed.

Function name indicates the identify of the function and parameter list indicates the names and types of variables used in that particular function. The variables must be separated by a comma. Function declaration is generally done in the global declaration section of the program.

Function call

A function is called in the place wherever the task has to be performed.

Syntax:

Variable = function name (parameters);

Where variable and parameters are optional based on the type of the function.

Parameters indicates the values on which the functions is to be performed. These parameters in the function call are called actual parameters. Variable here is used to store the value returned by the function.

Function definition

This is the part where the code for the function is written.

Syntax:

```
data type function name (parameters)
{
        local variable declaration;
        function body;
        return statement;
}
```

Hence, the parameter list indicates the arguments which take values from the actual arguments of function call and are called formal parameters.

Local variables declaration indicates declaration of variables that are used in that particular function.

Return statement is used to return a value from the function definition to the function call.

Note: *The values from actual arguments of function call are passed to formal parameters of function definition.*

Functions can be of different types:
1. Functions without parameters, without return value.
2. Functions with parameters, with return value.
3. Functions with parameters, without return value.
4. Functions without parameters, with return value.

Functions with parameters, with return value

These are the functions which pass values from functions call to function definition and take the return value from called function to the calling function.

Example :program:

```c
int sum (int a,  int b);
void main ( )
{
int x,y,z;
printf (" Enter any 2 values");
scanf ("%d%d", &x,&y);
z=sum(x,y);   /* function call*/
printf("sum is %d", z);
}
int sum (int a,  int b)
{
int c;/* Local variable declaration*/
    c=a+b;
    return (c);
}
```

Function with parameters, without return value

In these functions, values are passed from calling function to the called functions but no value is returned from called function to calling function.

The representation of no return value is done with the data type '
void'.

Example prog:
```
void sum (int a, int b);
void main ( )
{
int x,y;
printf (" Enter any 2 values");
scanf ("%d%d", &x,&y);
    sum(x,y);
}
void sum (int a, int b)
{
int c;
c=a+b;
printf("sum=%d",c);
}
```

Functions without parameters, with return value

These are the functions which do not take any values from the calling
function but return value to it.

Example prog:
```
int sum ( );
void main ( )
{
            int z;
        z=sum(x,y);
        printf("sum=%d",z);
}
int sum ()
{
   int a,b;
   printf("enter 2 values");
   scanf("%d%d",&a,&b);
```

```
        return(a+b);
        }
```

iv) Functions without parameters, without return value:
Functions without parameters indicate that no value are passed from
calling function to the called function and no return value indicates that
the called function will not give any data back to the calling function.

```
Example prog:  void sum ( );
               void main ( )
               {
               clrscr( );
                       sum(x,y);
               getch( );
               }
               void sum ()
               {
               int a,b;
               printf("enter 2 values");
               scanf("%d%d",&a,&b);
               printf("sum=%d",(a+b));
               }
```

Local variables & Global variables

These are two types of variables.
   a) Local Variables
   b) Global Variables.

a) Local Variables:
The variables declared inside a function are known as local variables.
The values of these variables cannot be accessed by any other
function.

Example:

```
void sum (int a, int b)
     {
          int z;
          z=a+b;
    return (z);
       }
```

Here z is a Local Variable which is declared in the function sum. So, the value of z is restricted to the function sum.

Example program:

```
void main()
{
int a=1,b=2;
clrscr();
printf("in main( ),
a=%d,b=%d",a,b);
fun( );
}
void fun()
{
int a=6,b=5;
printf("in fun( ),a=%d,b=%d",a,b);
}
```

b) *Global Variables:*

The variables declared outside the main( ) function are known as global variables. These variables can be accessed by all the functions of the program.

Example program:

```
int a=3,b=4;
void main( )
{
clrscr( );
printf("in main(), a=%d,b=%d",a,b);
a++;
b++;
```

```
fun ( );
}
void fun ( )
{
printf ("in fun ( ),a=%d,b=%d",a,b);
}
```

Parameter Passing

The technique of passing data from one function to another is known as parameters passing. Parameter passing can be done in two ways:

1. Call by value.
2. Call by reference.

1. *Call by value:*

Here, the values of actual parameters are passed to the variables in the parameters list of called function. The called function works on these formal parameters but not the actual parameters. So, any changes made in the formal parameters cannot effect the actual arguments.

Example program:
```
#include<stdio.h>
#include<conio.h>
        void swap(int,int);
void main ( )
{
int a,b;
printf ("enter any two values\n");
scanf ("%d%d",&a,&b);
swap (a,b);
}
void swap(int x,int y)
{
int t;
t=x;
```

```
     x=y;
     y=t;
     printf("after interchange\n");
     printf("%d  %d",x,y);
     }
```

2. *Call by reference:*

Here, the memory addresses of the variables are passed to the called function. The called function directly works on the data of the calling function. So, any changes made in the formal arguments will be reflected on the actual arguments.

The parameters receiving the addresses should be declared as pointer variables.

Example:

```
     int   *p;
```

Here, p indicates an address of an integer value.

Example program:

```
#include<stdio.h>
     #include<conio.h>
          void swap(int *,int *);
     void main( )
     {
int a,b;
printf("enter any two values\n");
scanf("%d%d",&a,&b);
swap(&a,&b);
                         printf("after
interchange\n");
printf("%d  %d",a,b);
getch( );
}
void swap(int *x,int *y)
{
int t;
t=*x;
```

```
*x=*y;
*y=t;
}
```


Storage Classes

Not only data type is required to declare a variable but its storage class also has to be mentioned. A storage class tells us four things:

(i)   Where the variable would be stored.
(ii)   Scope of the variable i.e., in which region of the program the value of the variable is available.
(iii)   Life of the variable i.e., how long the variable i.e., how long the variable would be active in the program.
(iv)   The initial value of the program if it is not initialized.

The storage classes available are:
1. Automatic
2. External
3. Static
4. Register.

1) ***Automatic variables*** are defined inside a function. A variable declared inside a function without a storage class name, by default is an auto variable.
The features of automatic variables are:

(i) Storage   : memory
(ii) initial value   : garbage (or) unpredictable
(iii) scope   : within the function
(iv) Life time   : till the control remains in the function.

These variables are created when the function is called and destroyed automatically when the function is exited.

Automatic variables are local to the function in which they are declared. These values cannot be accessed by any other function. The keyword used is 'auto'.

Example program:

```
void main( )
{
incr( );
incr( );
incr( );
}
void incr( )
{
auto int  x;
x=x+1;
printf("%d",  x);
}
```

2) *External variables* are also known as global variables. These variables are declared outside the function and the values of these variables are available to all the functions of the program.

Unlike Local Variables, Global Variables can be accessed by any function in the program. If sthe ame name is given to both the global and local variables priority is given to the local variable. The keyword " extern" is used to declare these variables.

The features of external variables are:

(i) Storage	: memory
(ii) initial value	: zero
(iii) scope	: Global
(iv) Life time	: till the program comes to an end.

3) *Static variables* may be of Local (or) global depending upon where it is declared. If it is declared outside the function, it is static global otherwise if it declared inside a function block, it is static local. A static variable is initialized only once and can never be re-initialized. The value of static variable persists at each call and last change made in the variable remains throughout the program execution.

The features of a static variable are:

(i) Storage   : memory
(ii) initial value   : zero
(iii) scope   : Local to the block in which variable is defined.
(iv) Life time   : persists till the end of program execution.

Example program:

```
void main( )
{
incr( );
incr( );
incr( );
}
void incr( )
{
static int x;
x=x+1;
printf("%d", x);
}
```

The keyword used to declare these variables is "static".

4) *Register Variables*: Instead of strings in memory, variables can also be stored in the register of cpu. The advantage of storing in registers is register access is faster than memory access, so, generally frequently accessed variables are kept in registers for foster execution of the program.

The features of register variables are:

(i) Storage   : Registers
(ii) initial value   : Garbage
(iii) scope   : Local
(iv) Life time   : un till the control remains in that function block.

Example:

```
void main( )
{
        register int i;
        for (i=1; i<=5; i++)
        printf (" %d/t", i);

}
```

Block Structure: In 'c', variables can be defined in a block-structured fashion within a function. Declaration of variables may follow the left brace that starts any compound statement. Variables declared inside a block are not affected by identically named variables in outer blocks. An automatic variable is initialized every time when the block is entered whereas a static variable is initialized only once at the time it enters the block.

Example program:

```
void main( )
{
int i=4;
if(i>3)
{
int i=3;
printf("%d", i);
}
printf("%d", i);
}
void main()
{
int j,i=4;
for(j=0;j<3;j++)
{
static int i=3;
printf("%d", i);
i++;
}
```

```c
            printf("%d", i);
            }
```

Recursive Functions

Recursion is a special case of process, where a function calls itself. A function is called recursive if a statement within the body of a function calls the same function.

```c
            factorial(x)
                    int x;
                    {
                    if (x = =1)
                    return(1);
                    else
                    return(x * factorial(x-1));
                    }
```

When writing recursive functions, you must have an If statement somewhere in the recursive function to force the function to return without out recursive call being executed. If you do not do this and you call the function, you will fall in an indefinite loop, and will never return from the called function.

Program to find factorial of a given number using a Recursive function

```c
#include<stdio.h>
int factorial(x)
int x;
{
  if (x<=1)
     return(1);
  else
     return(x*factorial(x-1));
}
main()
{
```

```c
int n,fn;
clrscr();
printf("enter n");
scanf("%d",&n);
fn=factorial(n);      /* Function Call */
printf("the factorial %d is %d\n",n,fn);
getch();
}
```

In case the value of n is 4, main() would call factorial() with 4 as its actual argument, and factorial() will send back the computed value. But before sending the computed value, factorial() calls factorial() and waits for a value to be returned.

```
factorial(4)  returns  4*factorial(3)
factorial(3)  returns  3*factorial(2)
factorial(2)  returns  2*factorial(1)
factorial(1)  returns  1
```

$4*6 = 24$
$3*2 = 6$
$2*1 = 2$
Back
substitution

A Program to find factorial of a given number using recursion.

```c
#include<stdio.h>
#include<conio.h>
int factorial(int);
void main( )
{
int n,k;
printf("enter any number\n");
scanf("%d",&n);
k=factorial(n);
printf("factorial of  %d is %d",n,k);
getch( );
}
int factorial(int x)
{
int fact;
if(x==0||x==1)
```

```c
return(1);
else
{
fact=(x*factorial(x-1));
return(fact);
          }
}
```

A Program to print fibonacii series using recursion.

```c
#include<stdio.h>
#include<conio.h>
int fib(int);
Void main()
{
    int i,n;
    printf("enter limit\n");
    scanf("%d",&n);
    for(i=1;i<=n;i++)
    printf("%d ",fib(i));
    getch( );
}
int fib(int x)
{
    if(x==1)
    return 0;
    else if(x==2)
    return 1;
    else
    return(fib(x-1)+fib(x-2));
}
```

Header Files

In 'c, a number of pre-defined functions are available to perform various tasks. To use these functions, we have to include the corresponding header file in which the function is available.

1. <u>stdio.h</u>: (standard input output library functions).
When any of the functions getchar ( ), qets ( ), putchar ( ), puts ( ), scanf( ), printf ( ) is used the header file stdio.h has to be included.

2. <u>math.h</u>: (mathematical functions)

1. *pow ():* This function returns x^n value.
Syntax:
```
pow (x,n);
```
Example:
```
pow (5,3)=5³=125.
```

3. *sqrt ():* This function performs square root of the given number.
Syntax:
```
sqrt (n);
```
Example:
```
sqrt (81)=9.
```

4. *log ():* This function returns natural logarithm of the given number.
Syntax:
```
log (n);
```
Example:
```
log (8);
```

4. *log10 ():* This functions returns logarithm value of the given number to the base 10.
Syntax:
```
log10 (n);
```

Example:

```
log10(10)=1
```

5. *exp( ):*This function returns e^r value.

Syntax:

```
exp (x);
```

Example:

```
exp(3);
```

6. *ceil ( ):* This function returns the next higher integer value of the given number.

Syntax:

```
ceil(n);
```

Example:

```
ceil (17.7)=18
ceil (1b.1)=17.
```

7. *floor( ):* This function returns the integer value less than or equal to the given number.

Syntax:

```
floor (n);
```

Example:

```
floor (17.7) = 17
        floor(16.1) = 16.
```

Cos, acos, cosh, sin, asin, sinh, tan, atan, tanh are also the functions under this header file.

3. <u>Stdlib.h</u>: (standard Library functions header file)

(i) *abs( ):* This functions returns the absolute value of a given, integer.

Syntax:

```
abs (integer value);
```

Example:

```
abs (-17); =17.
```

(ii) *fabs( ):* This functions returns absolute value (modulus) of a given floating point number.

Syntax:

```
fabs (float value);
```

Example:

```
fabs (-17.6) = 17.6.
```

(iii) *ato i ( ):* This function converts the given string to an integer value.

Syntax:

```
atoi(string);
```

Example:

```
atoi ("123") =123.
```

(iv) *atof ( ):* This function converts the given string into floating point value.

Syntax:

```
atof (string);
```

Example:

```
atof (" 123.56") = 123.560000.
```

4. <u>ctype. h:</u> (character testing and conversion functions)

(i) *isalpha( ):* This function checks whether the given character is an alphabet (or) not.

If it is an alphabet, it returns a non-zero value and otherwise a zero value.

Syntax:

```
is alpha ('a');          →          True
```

Example:

```
isalpha ('a')          →          True (non-zero)
isalpha ('2')          →          Flase (zero)
```

(ii) *isalnum( ):* This function checks whether the given character is an alphabet or a number. If true it returns a non-zero value other wise a zero value.

Example:
```
isalnum('1')      ->    True   (non-zero)
isalnum('q')      ->    False  (zero)
```

(iii) *isdigit ( ):* This function checks whether the given character is a digit or not. If true it returns a non-zero value otherwise a zero value.

Example:
```
isdigit ('a')    ->    True    (non zero)
isdigit('*')     ->    False  (zero)
```

(iv) *islower ( ):* This function checks whether the given character is a Lower case alphabet or not. If it is a small letter it returns a non-zero value otherwise a zero value.

Example:
```
islower ('b')  -> True (non-zero)
islower ('A')  -> False (zero)
```

(v) *isupper ( ):*This function checks whether the given character is a upper case alphabet or not. If it is a capital letter is returns a non-zero value otherwise a zero value.

Example:
```
isupper('B')     ->    True   (non-zero)
isupper('q')     ->    False  (zero)
```

(vi) *toupper ():* This function converts the given small letters to an upper case letter.

Example:
```
toupper ('b')=B
toupper('q')=Q
```

(vii) *tolower ():* This function converts the given capital letters to a Lower case letter.

Example:
```
tolower ('B') =b
tolower ('Q')=q
```

(viii) *toascii( ):*This function returns the equivalent ASCII value for the given character.

Example:
```
toascii('a') = 97
toascii('B') = 66
```

'C' Pre-Processor

A pre-Processor is a program that processes the source code before it passes through the compiler. It operates under the control of preprocessor directives preprocessor directives are placed in the program before the main line. All of the preprocessor directives begin with a # and do not end with a semicolon.

There are 3 types of pre-processor directives in 'C':

1. Macro Substitution directives
2. File inclusion directives.
3. Compiler control directives.

1. Macro Substitution directives:

Macro Substitution is a process of replacing an identifier by a pre-defined string. This is done by # define statement. This statement is known as macro.

Syntax: # define identifier string.

The string may be any text but the identifier must be a valid 'C' name.

A macro substitution can be of different forms:

a. Simple macro substitution.
b. Argument macro substitution.

c. Nested macro substitution.

a) Here the identifier is replaced by a simple string.

Example: # define PI 3-142

define TRUE 1

A macro definition can also include expressions.

Example: # define c(5*2+1)

To avoid incorrect results, the expression should always be enclosed with in parenthesis. A macro definition can also include any meaningful text.

Example:

```
# define MAIN main (  )   {
# define SUM (a+b)
# define PRINT printf("%d", sum);
# define END }
    MAIN
    int a,b;
    SUM;
    PRINT;
    END
```

b) Parameters can also be passed while defining a macro.

Example:

```
#define square (x)    ((x)*(x))
#define max (a,b)((a)x(b))) ? (a): (b))
     main ( )
     {
     int a=5,b=6;
     printf (" %d", max (a,b));
     }
```

c) One macro definition can be used in defining another macro.

Example:

```
#define square (x)     ((x)*(x))
# define cube(x)   (square (x) * (x))
```

There is also a possibility to undefined a macro. This is done by using the statement.

```
# undef identifier
```

This is useful when we want to restrict our definition only to a particular part of a program.

2. File inclusion directives:
A file containing macro definitions or function definitions can be included in a program so as to avoid rewriting the code.
This is done by the following preprocessor directive.

```
#  include "filename"
```

Here filename indicates the file containing the definitions.
This can be done in the following form

```
#  include <filename>
```

The difference is, in this case, the file is searched only in the standard directories as when we include the filename in double quotes it is searched in the current directory also.

3. Compiler Control Directives:
Compiler control directives are useful to activate or deactivate a group of lines in a program. They are,

```
# ifdef
#ifndef
#endif
#else
```

Example:

```
#include "file.c"
#ifdef PI 3.14
printf ("%d%d", TRUE, FALSE);
# else
printf ("%d", PI);
# end if
}
```

Functions Using Arrays

As values of variables can be passed to a function it is also possible to use array values in a function. To pass a one-dimensional array to a function, it is sufficient to list the name of the array without any subscripts and size of the array as arguments.

Example: sum (a,n);

Where a is the array name and n is the size of the array. But in function header, we need to mention the array as a subscripted variable.

Example: `sum (int a[ ], int n)` →t is not necessary to specify the size here.

A Program to print the maximum and minimum elements in a list of elements.

```
void arr_min(int a[ ],int n);
void arr_max(int a[ ],int n);
#include<stdio.h>
#include<conio.h>
void main( )
{
int i,n,a[10];
clrscr( );
printf("enter size of the array");
scanf("%d",&n);
printf("enter elements");
for(i=0;i<n;i++)
scanf("%d",&a[i]);
arr_min(a,n);
arr_max(a,n);    ( );
}
void arr_min(int a[ ],int n)
{
int i,min;
min=a[0];
for(i=1;i<n;i++)
{
if(min>a[i])
min=a[i];
}
```

```c
printf("minimum element is %d",min);
}
void arr_max(int a[ ],int n)
{
int i,max;
max=a[0];
for(i=1;i<n;i++)
{
if(max<a[i])
max=a[i];
                    }
printf("maximum element is %d",max);
          }
```

3. Arrays, Pointers and Strings

Objective

1. Provides knowledge of algorithms and flowcharts.
2. Teaches how to structure C programming.
3. Enhances understanding of the concepts of tokens, variables, data types, and their respective sizes.
4. Covers control statements in C programming.

This chapter serves as a comprehensive exploration of three foundational pillars in programming: Arrays, Pointers, and Strings. Arrays, structured repositories of data, initiate our journey, offering an ordered approach to storing and accessing multiple values within a single variable. As we traverse through their systematic arrangement, we uncover the efficiency and adaptability that arrays bring to tasks such as data manipulation and algorithmic solutions. The narrative seamlessly transitions to Pointers, agile navigators within the expansive memory landscape of a program. Pointers redefine memory management, enhancing data access efficiency and introducing dynamic memory allocation for flexible data structures. Our exploration culminates with Strings, dynamic sequences of characters crucial for text manipulation. Unravelling the intricacies of string handling, we delve into their storage, manipulation, and diverse applications—from straightforward text processing to intricate parsing tasks. Together, Arrays, Pointers, and Strings form a symphony of structured data representation and manipulation, shaping the very essence of efficient and expressive programming solutions within the chapters of this exploration.

Array

An array is a group of related data items that share a common name and stored in contiguous memory locations. Ordinary variables are capable of holding only one value at a time. However, there are situations in which we would be wanting to store more than one value at a time in a single variable.

For example, suppose we wish to arrange the percentage of marks obtained by 100 students in ascending order. In such a case we have two options to store these marks in memory.

1. Construct 100 variables to store percentage marks obtained by 100 different students.
2. Construct one variable capable of storing or holding all the hundred variables.

Obviously the second alternative is better. A simple reason for this is, it would be much easier to handle one variable than handling 100 different variables.

Array declaration

Like any other variable, arrays must be declared before they are used. The general form of array declaration is

        type variable-name [size];

The type specifies the type of element that will be contained in the array, such as int, float or char. Size indicates the maximum number of elements that can be stored inside the array.

For example

    1)   int number[5];
        Declares an array number which can store a maximum of 5 integer numbers.

    2)   float height[50];
        Declares an array height which can store a maximum of 50 floating-point numbers.

3)   char name[10];

Declares an array name which can store a maximum of 10 characters.

If we want to represent a set of five numbers say (35, 40, 20, 57, 19) by an array variable number, then we may declare the variable number as follows.

int number [5];

The computer reserves five storage locations as shown below. We know that memory is group of memory cells. Each cell can store one byte of information and each cell is accompanied with some address.

	Number [0]
	Number [1]
	Number [2]
	Number [3]
	Number [4]

The values to the array elements can be assign as follows.

```
number[0]=35;
number[1]=40;
number[2]=20;
number[3]=57;
number [4]=19;
```

This would cause the array number to store the values as shown below.

35	number[0]
4	number[1]
20	number[2]
57	number[3]
19	number[4]

The subscript of an array can be integer constant or integer variable.

Accessing Elements of An Array

Once an array is declared, the individual elements of the array can be referred by the use of subscript. Subscript specifies the element position in the array. Subscript starts at 0. i.e. first number is started at position 0, second number is started at position 1 etc.

Entering data into an array

```
int num [10];
for (i=0; i<10; i++)
{
        Printf ("enter a number");
        Scanf ("%d", & num [i]);
}
```

Reading data from an array

To add the elements of an array to variable sum

```
sum=0;
for (i=0; i<10; i++)
sum = sum + a [i];
```

1. An array is a collection of similar elements.
2. First element is at position '0', so the last element is at position 1 less then the size of the array.
3. An array is also known as subscripted variable.
4. Before using an array its type and dimension must be declared.
5. The elements are always stored in contiguous memory locations

Initialization of arrays

We can initialize the elements of an array in the same way as the ordinary variables when they are declared.

```
Static type array-name [size] = {list of
values};
```
The values in the list are separated by commas. If the number of values in the list is less then the size, then only that many elements will be initialized. The remaining elements will be set to zero automatically.

```
Static int num [5] = {10, 20, 30, 40, 50};
Static char name[ ] = { 'j','o','h','n' };
```

There are two types of arrays:
1.One-dimensional arrays
2.Two-dimensional arrays.

One-dimensional arrays

A list of related data type items can be given one variable name using single subscript. Such variable is called single subscripted variable or one-dimensional array.

Syntax:
```
Datatype variable[size];
```

Example:
```
int salary[10];
float marks[100];
char ch[10];
```

A Program to initialize an array and display the values.

```
#include<stdio.h>
#include<conio.h>
void main ( )
{
    int i,n,a[5]={11,22,33,44,55};
    clrscr ( );
    for(i=0;i<5;i++)
```

```
                         printf("%d\n",a[i]);
                         getch( );
          }
```

A Program to enter elements in to an array and display them.

```c
#include<stdio.h>
#include<conio.h>
void main( )
{
int i,n,a[10];
clrscr( );
printf("enter size of the array");
scanf("%d",&n);
printf("enter elements");
for(i=0;i<n;i++)
scanf("%d",&a[i]);
printf("the elements are\n");
for(i=0;i<n;i++)
printf("%d\n",a[i]);
getch( );
}
```

A Program to find minimum and maximum elements of an array.

```c
#include<stdio.h>
#include<conio.h>
void main( )
{
int i,n,a[10],max,min;
clrscr( );
printf("enter size of the array");
scanf("%d",&n);
printf("enter elements");
for(i=0;i<n;i++)
scanf("%d",&a[i]);
max=a[0];
min=a[0];
for(i=1;i<n;i++)
{
if(max<a[i])
max=a[i];
if(min>a[i])
```

```c
min=a[i];
}
printf("the maximum element is %d,minimum
element is %d",max,min);
getch( );
}
```

A Program to print elements of an array in ascending order.

```c
#include<stdio.h>
#include<conio.h>
void main( )
{

int i,a[10],n,temp;
printf("enter size of the array\n");
scanf("%d",&n);
printf("enter elements\n");
for(i=0;i<n;i++)
scanf("%d",&a[i]);
for(i=0;i<n;i++)
{
for(j=i+1;j<n;j++)
{
if(a[i]>a[j])
{
temp=a[i];
a[i]=a[j];
a[j]=temp;
}
}
}
printf("Ascending order is\n");
for(i=0;i<n;i++)
printf("%d ",a[i]);
}
```

Two-dimensional array

So far we have looked at arrays with only one dimension. It is also possible for arrays to have two or more dimensions. The two dimensional array is also called a matrix.

Consider the following data table

	sub1	sub2	sub3	sub4
Student1	10	20	30	40
Student2	5	7	8	15
Student3	3	2	4	50

3×4

The table contains a total of 12 values, i.e in each line. We can think of this table as a matrix consisting of 3 rows and 4 columns. Each row represents the marks obtained in 4 subjects by a particular student. Each column represents the marks obtained in a particular subject.

In mathematics, we represent a particular value in a matrix by using two subscripts, such as v_{ij}. Here v denotes the entire matrix and v_{ij} refers to the value in the ith row and j^{th} column.

For example in the above table v_{23} refers to the value 50.

C allows us to define such tables of items by using two-dimensional arrays, the above table can be defined in C as

```
int  v[3][4];
```

General form:

```
Type array_name [row-size] [col-size];
```

Two-dimensional arrays are stored in memory as shown below.

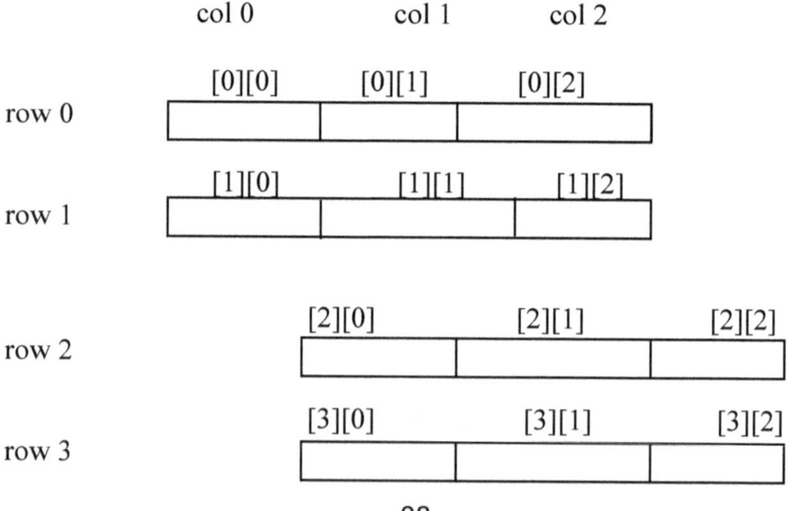

Unlike most other languages, which use one pair of parentheses with commas to separate array sizes, C places each size in its own set of brackets

Initializing two dimensional arrays

Like the one-dimensional arrays, two-dimensional arrays may be initialized by following their declaration with a list of initial values enclosed in braces.

```
Static int num [2][3] = {0, 0, 0, 1, 1, 1};
```

This declaration initiates the elements of first row to zero and second row to 1. The initialization is done row by row. The above statement is equivalently written as

```
Static    int    num    [2][3]    =    {{0,0,0},
{1,1,1}};
```

By surrounding the elements of each row by braces we can also initialize a two-dimensional array in the form of a matrix.

```
Static int num [2][3] = {
                        {0,0,0},
                        {1,1,1}
                };
```

If the values are missing in an initializer, they are automatically set to zero. For instance the statement

```
Static int num [2][3] = {
                        {1,1},
                        {2}
                };
```

will initialize the first two elements of the first row to one, the first element of the second row to two. And all other elements to zero.

Memory map of a two dimensional array:

```
Static int   num [2][3] = {1,2,3,4,5,6};
```

00	01	02	10	11	12
1	2	3	4	5	6

5002   5004 5006 5008 5010   5012

In memory whether it is a one-dimensional or a two-dimensional array the array elements are stored in one contiguous chain. The arrangement of array elements of a two-dimensional array in memory is shown above.

A Program to enter elements of a two-dimensional array and display them in matrix form.

```
#include<stdio.h>
#include<conio.h>
void main( )
{
int i,j,a[10][10],m,n;
pirntf("enter order of matrix\n");
scanf("%d%d",&m,&n);
printf("enter elements\n");
for(i=0;i<m;i++)
{
for(j=0;j<n;j++)
{
scanf("%d",&a[i][j]);
    }
}
printf("the elements in matrix form are\n");
for(i=0;i<m;i++)
{
for(j=0;j<n;j++)
{
 printf("%d\t",a[I][j]);
}
printf("\n");
}
}
```

A Program to perform addition of two matrices.

```
#include<stdio.h>
#include<conio.h>
void main( )
```

```c
{
int i,j,m,n,p,q,a[10][10],b[10][10],c[10][10];
clrscr( );
printf("enter order of first matrix");
scanf("%d%d",&m,&n);
printf("enter order of second matrix");
scanf("%d%d",&p,&q);
if(m==p&&n==q)
{
 printf("enter elements of first matrix");
for(i=0;i<m;i++)
for(j=0;j<n;j++)
scanf("%d",&a[i][j]);
printf("enter elements of second matrix");
for(i=0;i<m;i++)
for(j=0;j<n;j++)
scanf("%d",&b[i][j]);
for(i=0;i<m;i++)
{

for(j=0;j<n;j++)
{

c[i][j]=a[i][j]+b[i][j];
}
}
printf("the addition matrix is\n");
for(i=0;i<m;i++)
{
for(j=0;j<n;j++)
{
printf("%d\t",c[i][j]);
}
printf("\n");
}

  }
else
printf("addition is not possible");
getch( );
}
```

A Program to perform multiplication of two matrices.

```c
#include<stdio.h>
#include<conio.h>
void main( )
{
int
i,j,k,m,n,p,q,a[10][10],b[10][10],c[10][10];
clrscr( );
printf("enter order of first matrix");
scanf("%d%d",&m,&n);
printf("enter order of second matrix");
scanf("%d%d",&p,&q);
if(n==p)
{
printf("enter elements of first matrix");
for(i=0;i<m;i++)
for(j=0;j<n;j++)
scanf("%d",&a[i][j]);
printf("enter elements of second matrix");
for(i=0;i<m;i++)
for(j=0;j<n;j++)
scanf("%d",&b[i][j]);
for(i=0;i<m;i++)
{
for(j=0;j<q;j++)
{
c[i][j]=0;
for(k=0;k<p;k++)
{
c[i][j]+=a[i][k]*b[k][j];
}
}
}
printf("the resultant matrix is\n");
for(i=0;i<m;i++)
{
  for(j=0;j<q;j++)
  {
printf("%d\t",c[i][j]);
  }
printf("\n");
}
}
```

```c
else
printf("multiplication is not possible");
getch( );
}
```

A Program to check whether a matrix is symmetric or not.

```c
#include<stdio.h>
#include<conio.h>
void main( )
{
int i,j,a[10][10],m,n,at[10][10],count=0;
pirntf("enter order of matrix\n");
scanf("%d%d",&m,&n);
if(m==n)
{
        printf("enter elements\n");
        for(i=0;i<m;i++)
        {
                for(j=0;j<n;j++)
                {
                                scanf("%d",&a[i][j]);
                }
        }
for(i=0;i<m;i++)
{
        for(j=0;j<n;j++)
        {
                at[j][i]=a[i][j];
        }
}
        for(i=0;i<m;i++)
        {
                for(j=0;j<n;j++)
                {
                                if(a[i][j]!=at[i][j])
                                {
                                count++;
                                break;
                                }
                }
        }
```

```
if(count==0)
printf("matrix is symmetric");
else
printf("matrix is not symmetric");
}
      else
      printf("order is not same");
      getch( );
}
```

Multi-Dimensional Arrays

C language allows not only one-dimensional and two-dimensional arrays but also three or more dimensional arrays. A multi-dimensional array can be declared as follows:

Syntax:

```
      Datatype variable[size1][size2]……[size
n];
```

Example:

```
      Int a[3][3][3]={{{1,2,3},
            {4,5,6},
            {7,8,9}},
            {{10,11,12},
            {13,14,15}
            {16,17,18}},
              {{19,20,21},
             {22,23,24},
            {25,26,27}}};
```

A Program to read and print elements of a three dimensional array.

```
#include<stdio.h>
#include<conio.h>
void main( )
{
int i,j,k,a[10][10][10],m,n,p;
```

```c
pirntf("enter order of matrix\n");
scanf("%d%d",&m,&n,&p);
printf("enter elements\n");
for(i=0;i<m;i++)
{
for(j=0;j<n;j++)
{
for(k=0;k<p;k++)
{
scanf("%d",&a[i][j][k]);
}
}
}
printf("the elements in matrix form are\n");
for(i=0;i<m;i++)
{
for(j=0;j<n;j++)
{
for(k=0;k<p;k++)
{
printf("%d\t",a[I][j][k]);
 }
 printf("\n");
 }
 printf("\n");
 getch( );
}
```

Arrays and Functions

As values of variables can be passed to a function it is also possible to use array values in a function. To pass a one-dimensional array to a function, it is sufficient to list the name of the array without any subscripts and size of the array as arguments.

Example:
```c
        sum (a,n);
```

Where a is the array name and n is the size of the array. But in function header, we need to mention the array as a subscripted variable.

Example:

```
    sum (int a[ ], int n)
```

It is not necessary to specify the size here.

A Program to print the maximum and minimum elements in a list of elements.

```
void arr_min(int a[ ],int n);
void arr_max(int a[ ],int n);
#include<stdio.h>
#include<conio.h>
void main( )
{
int i,n,a[10];
clrscr( );
printf("enter size of the array");
scanf("%d",&n);
printf("enter elements");
for(i=0;i<n;i++)
scanf("%d",&a[i]);
arr_min(a,n);
arr_max(a,n);
getch( );
}
void arr_min(int a[ ],int n)
{
int i,min;
min=a[0];
for(i=1;i<n;i++)
{
if(min>a[i])
min=a[i];
}
printf("minimum element is %d",min);
}
void arr_max(int a[ ],int n)
{
int i,max;
max=a[0];
```

```c
for(i=1;i<n;i++)
{
if(max<a[i])
max=a[i];
}
printf("maximum element is %d",max);
}
```

Pointers

Definition: A pointer is a variable which is used to store address of another variable. Whenever a variable declaration is done, it tells the compiler three things.

For example: Consider the following declaration:
        int a=5;
It tells to
- (i)   reserve space in memory to hold the integer value.
- (ii)   Associate the name 'a' with this memory location
- (iii)   Store the value 5 at this location.

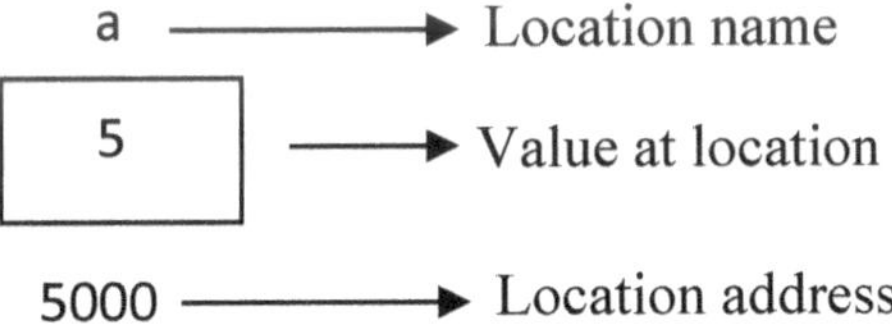

The address of a variable can be printed using the operator '&'. This is known as 'address of' operator.

Example:
```c
        void main( )
        {
                int a=5;
            printf("address of %d is %u", a, &a);
                }
```
where the control string %u denotes to print an unsigned integer.

NOTE: The '&' operator can be used only with a simple variable or an array element. It cannot be used with constants, array names and expression.

Example:

```
&45,
&(a+b),
int a[5];&a are illegal.
```

Declaration of pointers

Like normal variables, a pointer variable should also be declared before it is used. It can be done in the following form:

Syntax:

datatype *variablename;

Here, '*' is known as 'value at address' operator or indirection operator. It tells that the variable is a pointer variable. Datatype indicates the datatype of the value which is stored in the address location indicated by the pointer variable.

Example:

```
int *p;
```

It indicates that p is a variable, which stores the address of an integer value.

```
float *q;
```

It indicates that q is a variable, which stores the address of a float value.

```
char *r;
```

It indicates that r is a variable, which stores the address of a character value

Initialization of pointers:

Assigning address of some variable to a pointer is known as pointer initialization.

Example:
```
int x,*pt=&x;
void main( )
{
int *p,a=5;
p=&a;
pirntf("%d is at addres %u",a,p);
}
```

Accessing values of variables:

The value of a variable can be accessed in two ways. One way is to refer to the variable through its name and other way is to refer through the address location.

Example prog:
```
void main( )
{
int a=5,*p;
float b=2.5,*q;
char c='a',*r;
p=&a;
q=&b;
r=&c;
printf("a=%d, address of a=%u",*p,p);
printf("b=%d, address of b=%u",*q,q);
printf("c=%d, address of c=%u",*r,r);
}
```

NOTE: Whatever may be the datatype at the declaration of pointer variable, it takes 2 bytes of memory since the value of pointer variable is always an unsigned integer.

A Program to perform arithmetic operations using pointers.
```
#include<stdio.h>
#include<conio.h>
void main( )
{
        int a,b,*p1,*p2;
```

```
            p1=&a;
            p2=&b;
            printf("enter any two values");
            scanf("%d%d",&a,&b);
            printf("addition=%d",(*p1+*p2);
            printf("subtraction=%d",(*p1+*p2);
            printf("product=%d",(*p1+*p2);
            printf("division=%d",(*p1+*p2);
            getch( );
    }
```

A Program to interchange two values using pointers.

```
#include<stdio.h>
#include<conio.h>
void main( )
{
int a,b,&p1,&p2,t;
printf("enter any two values\n");
scanf("%d%d",&a,&b);
p1=&a;
p2=&b;
t=*p1;
*p1=*p2;
*p2=t;
printf("after interchange\n");
printf("%d  %d",a,b);
getch( );
}
```

Address Arithmetic

1. The only possible operation on two pointer variables Is subtraction. No other operation is possible. whenever a subtraction operation is performed on two pointer variable, it gives the number of values that can be stored between those two addresses.

Example:
```
    Int *p1,*p2;
```
Suppose p1=5000,p2=5040
Then, p2-p1=(5040-5000)=40/2=20.

i.e., 20 integer values can be stored between these two addresses.

Example:

```
float *p1,*p2;
```

Suppose p1=5000,p2=5040

Then, p2-p1=(5040-5000)=40/4=10.

i.e., 10 integer values can be stored between these two addresses.

Example:

```
char *p1,*p2;
```

Suppose p1=5000,p2=5040

Then, p2-p1=(5040-5000)=40/1=40.

i.e., 40 integer values can be stored between these two addresses.

2. Increment/decrement operations can be performed on pointer variables.

Example:

```
int *p1;
```

Let p1=5000

P1++; or ++p1;

The incrementation operation causes the pointer variable increments to length of the datatype which is known as scaling factor.

Hence, p1++ or ++p1 causes it to point to 5002. Since p1 is an integer pointer, an integer occupies 2 bytes, it increments by two locations. Similarly the decrement operation causes the variable to point to the address after subtracting the scaling factor.

Example:

```
Float *p1;
```

Let p1=5000

P1- -; or - -p1;

After the decrement operation, p1 points to 4996.Since here the scaling factor is 4. Likewise, the scaling factor for character is 1.

3. When we add any integer value to the pointer variable, the integer vlue gets multiplied with the scaling factor and corresponding number of bytes will be added.

Example:
```
int *p1;
```
Suppose p1=5000

P1+10=5000+10

=5000+(10*2)

=5020

Similarly, subtraction operation will be as follows:

Example:
```
float *p1;
```
Suppose p1=5000

P1-10=5000-10

=5000-(10*4)

=4960.

A Program for increment operation on pointers.
```
#include<stdio.h>
#include<conio.h>
void main( )
{
int a=5,*p1;
p1=&a;
float b=15.5,*p2;
p2=&b;
char c='a',*p3;
p3=&c;
printf("addresses are %u,%u,%u",p1,p2,p3);
printf("after incrementation\n");
p1++;
p2++;
p3++;
printf("addresses are %u,%u,%u",p1,p2,p3);
getch( );
}
```

Pointers to Arrays

Whenever an array is declared, the compiler allocates sufficient amount of storage locations to store all the elements of the array Example:

int a[5]={10,11,12,13,14};

	a[0]	a[1]	a[2]	a[3]	a[4]
	10	11	12	13	14
	5000	5002	5004	5006	5008

The address of first element of an array is called base address and this is stored in corresponding variable name.
i.e., a=&a[0]=5000.

The address of remaining elements can be found by simply adding the index value to the array name.

i.e., a+1=&a[1]=5002
    a+2=&a[2]=5004
    a+3=&a[3]=5006
    a+4=&a[4]=5008

The address of an array element can be calculate directly by using the formula:

```
address=base address+(index*scale factor)
```
Example:

address of a[3]=5000+3*2
=5006.

Whenever pointer to an array is declared, the pointer variable has to be initialized to the base address of the array.

Example:
```
int a[5],*pt;
```
Initialization can be done as:
```
pt=a; or pt=&a[0];
```

The address of remaining elements can be found by adding the index value to the pointer variable.
i.e., pt+1=&a[1]
    pt+2=&a[2]
    pt+3=&a[3]
    pt+4=&a[4]

The values of array elements can be accessed through *(pt+i). Where, I indicates the index of the array element. i.e., value of elements at base address =**pt;
*(pt+1)[a[1]
*(pt+2)[a[2]
*(pt+3)[a[3]
*(pt+4)[a[4]

*NOTE: *pt+i is different from *(pt+i). *pt+i adds I to the value at address pt, whereas *(pt+i) indicate4s the value at address (pt+i).*

A Program to print elements of an array using pointer to array.

```c
#include<stdio.h>
#include<conio.h>
void main( )
{
    int a[10],*pt,i,n;
    pt=a;
    printf("enter size of the
    array");
    scanf("%d",&n);
    prnitf("enter elements");
    for(i=0;i<n;i++)
    scanf("%d",pt+i);
    printf("the elements are");
    for(i=0;i<n;i++)
    scanf("%",*(pt+i));
    getch( );
}
```

A Program to print elements of an array in reverse order using pointer to array.

```c
#include<stdio.h>
#include<conio.h>
void main( )
{
```

```c
int a[10],*pt,i,n;
pt=a;
printf("enter size of the array");
scanf("%d",&n);
prnitf("enter elements");
for(i=0;i<n;i++)
scanf("%d",pt+i);
printf("the elements are");
for(i=n-1;i>=0;i--)
printf("%",*(pt+i));
getch( );
}
```

Pointers to 2D arrays

A pointer to a 2D array can be declared similar to a pointer to 1D array.

Example:

int a[2][3]={1,2,3,4,5,6};

a[0][0]	a[0][1]	a[0][2]	a[1][0]	a[1][1]	a[1][2]
1	2	3	4	5	6
5000	5002	5004	5006	5008	5010

The base address of the array has to be initialized to the pointer variable such as:

```
pt=a or pt=&a[0][0];
```

The address of an element can be caculated by the following formula:

```
Address=base address++columnsize*i+j
```

Where i indicates the row position and j indicates column position respectively.

Example:

Address of a[1][1]=5000+3*1+1
=5000+(4*2)
=5008.

A Program to read and print elements of 2D array using pointers.

```c
#include<stdio.h>
#include<conio.h>
void main( )
{
int a[10][10],*pt,i,j,m,n;
pt=a;
printf("enter size of the array");
scanf("%d",&n);
prnitf("enter elements");
for(i=0;i<m;i++)
for(j=0;j<n;j++)
scanf("%d",(pt+n*i+j));
printf("the elements are");
for(i=0;i<m;i++)
for(j=0;j<n;j++)
printf("%d\t",*(pt+n*i+j));
getch( );
}
```

Array of pointers

A pointer variable can store address of another variable whereas the array of pointers can store addresses of array elements. The pointer array can be declared as follows:
Syntax:
        Datatype *variable[size];
Example:
        Int *ap[10];

i.e., it indicates that ap is a pointer array which can store addresses of 10 elements which are of integer datatype.
A Program to print elements of an array and their corresponding addresses.

```c
#include<stdio.h>
#include<conio.h>
void main( )
{
    int a[5]={1,2,3,4,5},*ap[5],i;
```

```c
            for(i=0;i<5;i++)
            ap[i]=a+I;
            printf("the elements are");
            for(i=0;i<5;i++)
            printf("%d is at
            %u\n",*ap[i],ap[i]);
            getch( );
        }
```

Strings

Definition: A string can be defined as a group of characters, terminate with a NULL.

Since there is no separate datatype to declare strings, we declare a string as an array of characters using the datatype char.

Syntax:
```c
        Char variable[length];
```

Initialization of strings:

     A string can be initialized in different ways:

Example:
```c
        Char name[4]={'Q','I','S','\0'};
        Char name[]="QIS";
```
A string is always terminated by a NULL character '\0', which represents the end of the string.

Representation:

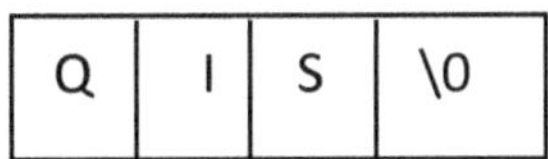

A string is an array of characters. Any group of characters defined between double quotation marks is a constant string.

Example:

     "c programming"

     "Rama is a good boy"

Declaration

        char   string name[size]

A string variable is any valid C variable and is always declared as an array. The size determines the number of characters in the string.

```
char    city[10];
char    name[20];
```

When the compiler assigns a character string to a character array. It automatically supplies a null character ('\0') at the end of the string. Therefore the size should be equal to the maximum number of character in the string plus one. Character array may be initialized when they are declared. C permits a character array to be initialized in either of the following two forms.

```
static char city [7] = {'g','u','n','t','u','r','\0'};
city[7] = "guntur";
```

The reason that city had to be 7 elements long is that the string 'guntur' contains 6 characters and one element space is provided for the null terminator.

C also permits us to initialize a character array without specifying the number of elements. In such cases, the size of the array will be determined automatically based on the number of elements initialized. For example

```
Static char string [] = {'g','o','o','d','\0'}
```
defines the array string as a five element array.

Reading strings from terminal

The input function scanf() can be used with %s format specification to read in a string of characters.

```
Char   address[15];
Scanf("%s",address);
```

The problem with scanf() function is that it terminates its input on the first white space it finds. (A white space includes blanks, tabs, carriage return, form feeds, new line). Therefore if the following line of text is typed in at the terminal

New York

Then only the string 'new' will be read into the array address, since the blank space after the word 'new' will terminate the string.

Note that unlike previous scanf calls, in the case of character arrays, the ampersand (&) is not required before the variable name.
The scanf() function automatically terminates the string that is read with a null character and therefore the character array should be large enough to hold the input string plus the null character.

Reading a line of text

In many texts processing applications, we need to read in an entire line of text from the terminal. It is not possible to use scanf() function to read a line containing more than one word. This is because the scanf terminates reading as soon as a space is encountered in input.

We can use getchar() function repeatedly to read successive single characters from the input and place them into a character array. Thus an entire line of text can be read and stored in an array. The reading is terminated when the new line character '\n' entered and the null character is then inserted at the end of the string.

```c
/* Program to read a line of text from terminal */
main();
{
     char   line[81],ch;
     int   i;
     i=0;
     printf("enter   line   of   text
<return> at  end \n");
     do
       {
          ch=getchar();
          line[i]=ch;
          i++;
       } while(ch!='\n');
     i--;
     line[i]='\0';
     printf("%s", line);
}
```

program to copy one string to another and count the number of characters copied

```
main();
    {
        char  str1[80], str2[80];
        int  i;
        scanf("%s", str1);
        for(i=0; str[i]!='\0'; i++)
            str2[i] = str1[i];
            str2[i] ='\0';
        printf("str1=%s\n", str1);
        printf("str2=%s\n", str2);
        printf("no.of char=%d\n", i);
    }
```

Writing strings to screen

```
        printf("%s", name);
```

can be used to display the entire contents of the array name. We can also specify the precision with which the array is displayed for instance the specification.

$$\%10.4s$$

This indicates that the first four characters are to be printed in the field width of 10 columns. However, if we include the minus sign in the specification (Eg: %-10.4s), the string will be printed left justified.

Example - 1/* writing strings using %s format */

```
main();
{
static char name[8]="college";
printf("%8s\n",name);
printf("%4s\n",name);
printf("%8.4s\n",name);
printf("%-8.4s\n",name);
printf("%8.0s\n",name);
printf("%.4s\n",name);
printf("%s\n",name);
}
```

× college
collegex
××××coll
coll××××
××××××××
coll
collegex

Example – 2 Program to print a string as shown below

```
main()
{
static char str[]="cprogramming";
int i,d;
for(i=0; i<=11; i++)
{
d=i+1;
printf("%-12.*s\n", d, str);
}
for(i=11; i>=0; i--)
{
d=i+1;
printf("%-12.*s\n",d,string);
}
}
```

```
c
cp
cpr
cpro
:
:
:
cprogramming
cprogramming
cprogrammin
cprogrammi
:
:
:
cp
c
```

Rules
1. When the field width is less than the length of the string, the entire string is printed.
2. The integer value on the right side of the decimal point specifies the number of characters to be printed.
3. When the number of characters to be printed is specified as zero, nothing is printed.
4. The minus sign in the specification causes the string to be printed left justified.

```
printf("% .*s\n", w, d, str);
```

prints the first 'd' characters of string in the field width of w.

Arithmetic Operations on Characters

C allows us to manipulate characters the same way we do with numbers. Whenever a character constant or a character variable is used in an expression, it is automatically converted into an integer value.

```
x='a';
printf("%d\n",x);
```

will display the number 97 at the screen. It is also possible to perform arithmetic operations on character constants and variables.

$$x = 'z' - 1$$

is a valid statement. In ascii the value of 'z' is 122 and therefore the statement will assign the value 121 to variable x.

We may also use character constants in relational expressions   for example, the expression

$$ch >= 'A' \&\& ch <= 'Z'$$

would test whether the character contained in the variable character is an upper-case letter. We can convert a character digit to its equivalent integer value using the following relationship.

```
x=character –'0';
  =ASCII of'5' – ASCII of '0'
  =53 – 48
  =5.
```

```
int x;
char ch = '5';
x = ch – '0';
printf("%d",x);
```

(5)

C library supports a function that converts a string of digits into their integer values.

```
x = atoi(string);
number = "1988";
year = atoi(number);
printf("%d",year);
```

A Program to read a string and print it.

```
#include<stdio.h>
#include<conio.h>
Void main( )
{
char str[10];
int i;
printf("enter any string\n");
scanf("%s",str);
printf("the string is");
for(i=0;str[i]!='\0';i++)
printf("%c",str[i]);
getch( );
}
```

A Program to find length of a string.

```c
#include<stdio.h>
#include<conio.h>
void main( )
{
char str[10];
int count=0;
printf("enter any string");
scanf("%s",str);
for(i=0;str[i][!='\0';i++)
count++;
printf("length of the string is %d",count);
getch( );
}
```

A Program to reverse a string.

```c
#include<stdio.h>
#include<conio.h>
void main( )
{
char str[10],rev[10];
int I,count=0;
printf("enter any string");
scanf("%s",str);
for(i=0;str[i]!='\0';i++)
count++;
count--;
for(i=0;count>=0;i++,count--)
rev[i]=str[count];
rev[i]=NULL;
printf("reverse is %s",rev);
getch( );
}
```

String handling functions

1.**strlen( ):**This function is used to determine the length of a string.
syntax:
```c
        strlen(string);
```

Example:
```
#include<stdio.h>
#include<conio.h>
void main( )
{
        char name[10];
        int   length;
        printf("enter any string");
        scanf("%s",str);
        length=strlen(str);
        printf("length=%d",length);
        getch( );
}
```

2. strcpy( ): This function copies a string from source to destination.
syntax:
```
strcpy(destination,source);
```

Example: Program:
```
#include<stdio.h>
#include<conio.h>
void main( )
{
        char  str1[10],str2[10];
        printf("enter any string");
        scanf("%s",str1);
        strcpy(str2,str1);
        printf("after  copying  %s",str2);
}
```

3.strncpy( ): This function copies the specified number of characters from the source string to destination string.
syntax:
```
strncpy(destination,source,n);
```
Example: Program:
```
#include<stdio.h>
#include<conio.h>
void main( )
{
char  str1[10],str2[10];
int n;
printf("enter any string");
scanf("%s",str1);
```

```c
        printf("enter number of characters to be
copied");
      scanf("%d",&n);
      strncpy(str2,str1,n);
      printf("after  copying  %s",str2);
}
```

4.**strcmp( ):**This function compares two strings and returns 0 if the strings are same, other wise it returns the ascii value difference of the unmatched character.
syntax:
```c
      strcmp(string1,string2);
```
Example: Program:
```c
      #include<stdio.h>
      #include<conio.h>
      void main( )
      {
      char  str1[10],str2[10];
      int n;
      printf("enter any string");
      scanf("%s",str1);
      printf("enter second string");
      scanf("%s",str2);
      n=strcmp(str1,str2);
      if(n==0)
      printf("strings are same");
      else
      printf("strings are different");
      }
```
5.**stricmp( ):**This function is used to compare two strings independent of the case.
Syntax:Strcmp(string1,string2);

Example: Program:
```c
      #include<stdio.h>
      #include<conio.h>
      void main( )
      {
      char  str1[10]="WELCOME"
      char  str2[10]="welcome";
      int n;
      n=strcmp(str1,str2);
      if(n==0)
```

```
printf("strings are same");
else
printf("strings are different");
}
```

6.**strnicmp( ):**This function compares the given two strings up to n characters independent of the case.

Syntax: `Strnicmp(string1,string2,n);`

7.**strlwr( ):**This function is used to convert the upper case alphabet to its equivalent lower case.

Syntax: `strlwr(ch);`
Where ch represents any character.

8.**strupr( ):**This function is used to convert the lower case alphabet to its equivalent upper case.
Syntax: `strupr(ch);`
Where ch represents any character.

9.**strcat( ):**This function is used to concatenate two strings.

Syntax:
```
Strcat(string1,string2);
```

10.**strncat( ):**This function is used to concatenate n characters of one string to the second string.

Syntax:
```
Strncat(string1,string 2,n);
```

11.**strrev( ):**This function is used to reverse a string.

Syntax:
```
Strrev(string);
```

A Program to check whether a string is palindrome or not using string handling functions.

```
#include<stdio.h>
#include<conio.h>
```

```c
void main( )
{
    char str[10];
    clrscr( );
    printf("enter any string");
    scanf("%s",str);
    if(strcmp(str,strrev(str))==0)
    printf("the string is a
    palindrome");
    else
    printf("not palindrome");
    getch( );
}
```

Pointers and Strings

Operations on string can be performed in an easier way using pointers.

A String is a character array which is declared as follows.

```c
Char str [10];
```

Pointers to a string can be declared using a variable which holds base address of the string.

Pointers to a string can be declared as follows.

```c
Char *p;
```

The base address of a string can be stored in a pointer variable as follows.

```c
P=str;
```

Write a Program to read and display a string using pointers.

```c
#include<stdio.h>
#include<conio.h>
void main ()
{
    char str[10], *p;
    printf("enter any string");
    gets(str);
```

```c
    p=str;
    while(*p!='\0')
{
    printf("%c",*p)
    p++;
}
}
```

Write a Program to find length of a string using pointers.

```c
    #include<stdio.h>
    #include<conio.h>

    void main ()
      {
            char str[10], *p,*q;
            printf("enter any string");
            gets (str);
            p=str;
            q=p;
    while(*p!='\0')
    {
    p++;
    }
    printf("length=%d",p-q);
    }
```

Write a program to print reverse of a string using pointers.

```c
    #include<stdio.h>
    #include<conio.h>
    #include<string.h>
    void main ()
    {
    char str[10], *p, *q;
    printf("enter any string");
    gets(str);
    p=str;
    q=p;
    while(*p!='\0')
{
p++;
}
```

```c
p--;
while(p>=q)
{
printf("%c",*p);
p--;
}
}
```

Write a Program to perform concatenation of 2 strings using pointers.

```c
#include<stdio.h>
#include<conio.h>
#include<string.h>
void main()
{
char str1[10], str2[10];
int i,j;
printf("enter first string");
gets(str1);
printf("enter second string");
gets(str2);
p=str1;
for(i=0;  *(p+i)!='\0';i++);
for(j=0;  str2[j]!='\0';i++,j++)
{
    *(p+i)=str2[j];
}
    *(p+i)='\0';
puts(str2);
}
```

Pointers as function Arguments

Arguments can be passed to a function in 2 ways.

    (i)   call by value and

    (ii)   call by reference

In call be value, we pass values of actual arguments to the corresponding formal arguments. The changes in formal arguments do not reflect in actual arguments.

In call by reference, addresses of actual arguments are passed from calling function to the called function. The formal arguments that receive addresses are declared as pointers variable of same datatype. Here, the changes tha5t are made in formal arguments are reflected in the actual arguments also.

A Program to find the biggest of two numbers using pointers as function arguments.

```
#include<stdio.h>
#include<conio.h>
Int large(int *, int *);
void main()
{
    int x,y,z;
    printf("\n enter any 2 values");
    scanf("%d%d",&x,&y);
    z=large(&x,&y);
    printf("biggest=%d",z);
}
int large(int *p, int *q)
{
    if(*p>*q)
    return(*p)
    else
    return(*q);

}
```

A Program to print the array elements using pointers as function arguments.

```
#include<stdio.h>
#include<conio.h>
void array(int *);
void main()
{
int a[5]={1,2,3,4,5};
clrscr();
array(a);
}
```

```c
void array(int *x)
{
int i;
for(i=0;i<5;i++)
{
printf("%d",*x);
x++;
}
}
```

Pointers and Functions

Every variable in'c' has an address except register variable. We can access these addresses using pointers. Likewise, functions in 'c' also have addresses. The address of a function can be known by pointers to function.

A pointer to a function can be declared as follows.

```c
Data type (*function name)(parameter list);
```

Example:
```c
        int (*p) ( );
```

It indicates P is a pointer to a function which stores address of a function.

A Program to call a function using pointers.

```c
#include<stdio.h>
#include<conio.h>
void (*p) ( );
void show( );
     void main( )
     {
         p=show;
         (*p) ( );
     }
     void show
     {
         printf("address of function%u",show);
     }
```

Functions returning pointers

The way in which a function can return an integer, float or any other datatype, it can also return a pointer, it has to be mentioned explicitly. A function returning a pointer can be declared as follows:

```
Data type *function name(parameters);
```

Example:

```
    int *fun();
    void main()
{
    int *p;
    p=fun();
    printf("%u",p);
}

int *fun()
{
    int a=5;
    printf("address of a is");
    return(&a);
}
```

Here, the declaration int *fun(): indicates that fun() is a function without parameters but return an integer pointer.

Functions returning multiple values

Normally a function can return only one value at a time. But it is possible to make a function return multiple values at a time by using pointers.

Example:

```
    #include<stdio.h>
    #include<conio.h>
    int fun(int *, int *, int *, int *);
    void main()
{
```

```c
int x,y, sum, diff;
clrscr();
printf("\n enter any 2 values");
scanf("%d%d",&x,&y);
fun(&x, &y, &sum, &diff);
printf("sum=%d",sum);
printf("diff=%d",diff);
}
            int fun(int *a, int *b, int *c, int
    *d);
{
    *c=*a+*b;
    *d=*a-*b;
}
```

Pointers to Pointers

Pointers is a variable which contains address of another variable. Pointers variables also have an address. The pointer variable containing address of another pointer variable is called pointer to pointer.

Syntax:

```c
Data type **variable;
```

Example:

```c
int a=10;
int *p1=&a;
int **p2=&p1;
```

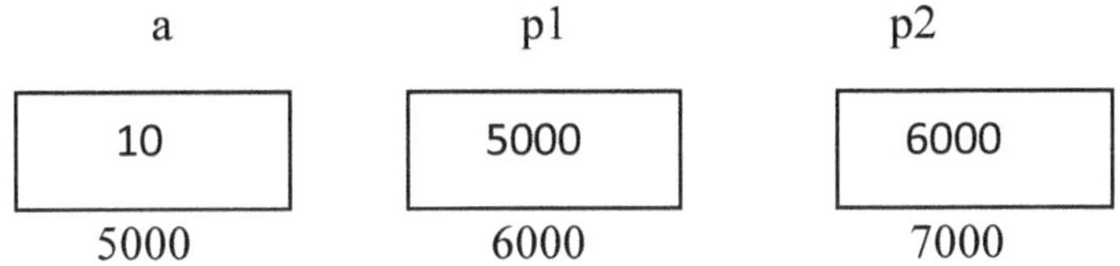

Here, p1 is a pointer variable which stores the address of a i.e., 5000. this is also stored in another address 6000. the variable p2 stores the address of a pointer p1. thus, p2 is known as pointer to pointer. Here the data type indicates the value that is stored in address of the pointer variable whose address is stored in pointer to pointer variable.

Thus, the chain of pointers can be extended to any extent.

Example: program:

```c
#include<stdio.h>
#include<conio.h>
void main()
{
  int a=5, *p1, **p2;
p1=&a;
p2=*p1;
printf("address of a =%u", p1);
printf("address of p1=%u",p2);
    printf("value of a=%d", **p2);
    }
```

Dynamic Memory Allocation

We can allocate memory to variables in two ways:
1. static memory allocation
2. dynamic memory allocation

Allocation of memory at the time or compilation is called static memory allocation.

Example: When an array is declared in a[10], it allocates 20 bytes of memory to store the integers but at runtime, we may or may not utilize it completely which results in wastage of memory. And moreover, it is also not possible to increase the size of memory during runtime. This disadvantage can be overcome by allocating the required memory at the time of execution. This allocating memory dynamically at the time of execution of program is called dynamic memory allocation. This can be done by standard functions (i) malloc and (ii) calloc.

malloc: It is a pre-defined function used to allocate memory dynamically.

Syntax:
```c
Pointer  variable=(datatype*)malloc(number  of
bytes required);
```

Here, the function malloc allocates memory for the byte size specified. It is converted to the pointer of datatype mentioned. It returns the address of first byte of the memory allocated which is assigned to the pointer variable. If the address allocation cannot be done, it returns NULL.

Example: ptr=(int*)malloc(10);
It allocates 10 bytes which stores integer values and the first byte address is stored in the pointer variable ptr.

A Program to implement malloc function.

```
#include<stdio.h>
#include<conio.h>
#include<alloc.h>
void main( )
{
    int i,n,*p;
    printf("enter number of
    elements");
    scanf("%d",&n);
    p=(int *)malloc(n*2);
    printf("enter elements");
    for(i=0;i<n;i++)
    scanf("%d",p+i);
    printf("the elements are\n");
    for(i=0;i<n;i++)
    printf("%d\n",p+i);
    getch( );
}
```

(i)   *calloc:* This is also a pre-defined function for dynamic memory allocation which slightly differs from the function malloc. calloc function contains two arguments. The first one specifies number of data items for which the memory has to be allocated and second argument specifies the number of bytes for each data item.

Syntax:
```
Pointer variable=(datatype*)calloc(number
of data items, size);
```

Example:
```
    ptr=(int *)calloc(10,2);
```
The above example allocates memory for 10 data items, 2 bytes for each data item and the address of starting location is stored in the variable ptr.

A Program to implement calloc function.

```
#include<stdio.h>
#include<conio.h>
#include<alloc.h>
void main( )
{
    float i,n,*p;
    printf("enter number of
    elements");
    scanf("%f",&n);
    p=(int *)calloc(n,4);
    printf("enter elements");
    for(i=0;i<n;i++)
    scanf("%f",p+i);
    printf("the elements are\n");
    for(i=0;i<n;i++)
    printf("%f\n",p+i);
    getch( );
}
```

(ii)   *realloc:* It is possible to increase or decrease already allocated memory by using this reallocation function.i.e., when once we allocate memory dynamically through malloc or calloc , the allocated block size can be increased or decreased by this function.

Syntax:
```
Pointer variable =(datatype*) realloc
(starting address of allocated memory, new
byte size required);
```

Example: `ptr=(int*)realloc(ptr,40);`

Here, the first argument of realloc function specifies the starting address of already allocated block and the second argument specifies the new size required. The new byte size may be larger or smaller than already allocated size. When it is smaller, i.e., when we decrease the size, there is no change in the base address of newly allocated block whereas when it its large, i.e., when we try to increase the size, then it first checks whether it is possible to extend the size without changing the base address. If it is not possible, it tries to allocate required memory somewhere else and after allocating the new block of memory, the contents are moved to new block and the new base address is stored in corresponding pointer variable.

A Program to implement realloc function.

```
#include<stdio.h>
#include<conio.h>
#include<alloc.h>
            void main( )
    {
int i,n,m,*p;
printf("enter number of elements");
scanf("%d",&n);
p=(int *)malloc(n*2);
printf("enter elements");
for(i=0;i<n;i++)
     scanf("%d",p+i);
printf("the elements and corresponding
addresses are\n");
for(i=0;i<n;i++)
printf("%d\t%u\n",*(p+i),p+i);
free(p);
printf("enter new size");
scanf("%d",&m);
p=(int*)realloc(p,2*m);
printf("enter elements");
for(i=0;i<m;i++)
     scanf("%d",p+i);
     printf("after reallocation\n");
printf("the elements and corresponding
addresses are\n");
for(i=0;i<m;i++)
printf("%d\t%u\n",*(p+i),p+i);
getch( );
    }
```

(iii)   ***free( ):*** The memory once allocated can be deallocated using this function.

Syntax:
```
free(starting address of allocated block);
```

Example: `free(ptr);`

Command Line Arguments

A command line argument is a parameter supplied to the program when the program is invoked. The parameters from command line can be passed to the program through two arguments in main function. They are argc,argv.

Argc: argc is an argument counter which contains the arguments on the command line.

Argv: argv is an argument vector which represent an array of character pointers that point to the command line arguments. The first argument should be the name of the program In order to access command line arguments ,we must declare main function and its parameters as follows:

Syntax:
```
void Main(argc,argv)
Example:
main(int argc,char *argv[])
int argc;
{
 Char argv[];
(or)
 /*body of the program*/
 {                                          }
 /*body of the  program*/
 }
```

A Program to print the arguments passed using the command line arguments

```
void main(argc,argv[])
int argc;
```

```c
char *argv[];
{
                int I;
                printf("number of
                arguments=%d",argc);
                printf("the arguments are\n");
                for(I=1;I<argc;I++)
                {
                    printf("%s\n",argb[I]);
                    }
                                getch( );
}
```

A Program to copy contents of one file to another using command line arguments

```c
#include<stdio.h>
#include<conio.h>
void main(
{
FILE *fs,*ft;
char ch;
fs=fopen("argv[1]","r");
if(fs==NULL)
{
printf("cannot open file");
exit(0);
            }
ft=fopen("argv[2]","w");
if(ft==NULL)
{
printf("cannot open file");
exit(0);
}
while((ch=getc(fs))!=EOF)
{
    putc(ch,ft);
}
fclose(ft);
printf(" the copied contents are \n");
ft=fopen("argv[2]", "r");
while((ch=getc(ft))!=EOF)
{
```

```
putchar(ch);
}
fclose(fs);
fclose(ft);
getch( );
}
```

4. Structures and Unions

Objective

1. Provides knowledge of algorithms and flowcharts.
2. Teaches how to structure C programming.
3. Enhances understanding of the concepts of tokens, variables, data types, and their respective sizes.
4. Covers control statements in C programming.

Within the scope of this chapter, our focus is on three pivotal constructs in programming: Structures, Unions, and Bitfields. We embark on an exploration of Structures, versatile entities that enable the encapsulation of diverse data types within a cohesive framework. As we navigate the organized architecture of structures, their role in enhancing code organization and facilitating the creation of sophisticated data structures becomes evident. The narrative seamlessly transitions to Unions, introducing a unique paradigm where different data types can share the same memory space. Unions offer a space-efficient solution for scenarios requiring flexibility in data interpretation. Further enriching our exploration is the inclusion of Bitfields, enabling precise control over individual bits within a data structure. Together, Structures, Unions, and Bitfields form a trio that not only shapes the efficiency of memory utilization but also empowers programmers with versatile tools for crafting optimized and intricate data representations. Join us in this chapter where we unravel the intricacies of these constructs, paving the way for a deeper understanding of organized and efficient data manipulation in programming.

Introduction to Structures

We have seen that arrays can be used to represent a group of data items that belong to the same type, such as int or float. However, if we want to represent a collection of data items of different types using a single name, then we can not use array. C supports a constructed data type known as structure, which is a method of packing data of different data types. A structure is a convenient tool for handling a group of logically related data items.

Definition: A structure is a collection of one or more members of different data types grouped together under a single name.

An array can store more number of elements that belong to same datatype but by using a structure we can store number of elements each of different datatype under the same name.

Declaration of a structure

A structure can be declared as follows:
Syntax:

```
Struct tag name
{
        data member 1;
        data member 2;
        :
        :
        data member n;
};
```

The keyword struct is used to declare a structure. The tagname indicates the name of the structure. member 1,member 2,……up to member n are the members of different datatypes which are to be stored under the tagname. The structure declaration should always terminate with a semicolon. The members are not variables by themselves. The members are used to indicate the different datatypes of information that is stored under the tagname.

Declaration of a structure variables

To access the members of a structure, structure variables are to be declared after the declaration of a structure.
Example:

```
struct student
{
        char name[10];
        int rollno;
        float avg;
```

};
struct student s1;
where s1 is the structure variable which occupies 16 bytes(10 for name, 2 for rollno, 4 for avg).
The structure declaration and variable declaration can be combined as follows:

```
Struct student
{
        char name[20];
        int rollno;
        float avg;
}s1;
```

Initialization of a structure

A structure can be initialized as follows:
        Struct tagname variable={values separated with commas};

        Where order of initialization should be same as order of member declaration.
Example:struct student s1={"ramya",20,80.5};

        The values can be initialized to the variables using dot operator(.).

        Syntax: Variablename.member name=value;
        Example: s1.rollno=5;
Dot operator is also known as member operator or period operator.

A Program to initialize the structure and display the details.

```
void main()
{
struct book
{
char name[10];
int pages;
float price;
};
struct book b1={"c& ds",250,150.5};
 printf("name=%s",b1.name);
```

```
printf("pages=%d",b1.pages);
printf("price=%f",b1.price);
getch();
}
```

A Program to initialize the structure details individually and display them.

```
void main()
{
struct book
{
char name[10];
int pages;
float price;
}b1;
strcpy(b1.name,"c& ds");
b1.pages=250;
b1.price=150.5;
 printf("name=%s",b1.name);
 printf("pages=%d",b1.pages);
 printf("price=%f",b1.price);
 getch();
}
```

A Program to enter and print details of a structure.

```
void main()
{
struct book
{
char name[10];
int pages;
float price;
};
struct book b1;
printf("enter details\n");
scanf("%s,b1.name);
scanf("%d",&b1.pages);
scanf("%f",&b1.price);
printf("the details are\n");
 printf("name=%s",b1.name);
```

```c
printf("pages=%d",b1.pages);
printf("price=%f",b1.price);
getch();
}
```

A Program to copy values of one structure variable to another.

```c
void main()
{
struct employee
{
char name[10];
int age;
 float salary;
}
e2;
struct employee e1={"Ajay",30,5000.5};
strcpy(e2.name,e1.name);
e2.age=e1.age;
e2.salary=e1.salary;
 printf("employee 2 details are\n");
 printf("name=%s\nage=%d\nsalary=%f",e2.anme,e2.age,e2.salary);
getch();
}
```

A Program to compare values of two structure variables.

```c
void main()
{
struct student
{
int rollno;
char grade;
 float avg;
}s1,s2;
printf("enter details of first student\n");
scanf("%d%c%f",&s1.rollno,&s1.grade,&s1.avg);
printf("enter details of second student\n");
scanf("%d%c%f",&s2.rollno,&s2.grade,&s2.avg);
if(s1.rollno==s2.rollno&&s1.grade==s2.grade&&s1.avg=s2.avg)
printf("s1 and s2 are same");
else
```

```
printf("different");
}
```

Pointers to Structures

We know that pointer is a variable which holds address of a variable (int or float or any datatype)or address of a function. Similarly a pointer to a structure can also be defined which holds the base address of structure member variable.
A pointer to a structure can be declared as follows:

```
Struct tagname *variable;
```

Example:

```
            struct book
            {
                    char name[10];
                    int pages;
                    float price;
            };
            struct book *ptr;
```

The members of the structure can be accessed through pointer variable using arrow operator(->)which is also known as member selection operator.

The members of the structure book can be accessed as:

```
        Ptr->name
        Ptr->pages
        Ptr->price
```

A Program on pointers to structures

```
void main()
{
struct student
{
char name[10];
int rollno;
float avg;
};
```

```c
struct student s1={"Ajay",5,80.5};
struct student *ptr;
ptr=&s1;
printf("name=%s\n"ptr->name);
printf("rollno=%d\n",ptr->rollno);
printf("avg=%f",ptr->avg);
}
```

Arrays of Structures

We use structures to describe the format of a number of related variables. For example, in analyzing the marks obtained by a class of students, we may use a template to describe student name, marks obtained in various subjects and then declare all the students as structure variables. In such cases, we may declare an array of structures, each element of the array representing a structure variable.

```c
Struct    class    student[100];
```

Defines an array called student that consists of 100 elements. Each element is defined to be of the type struct class.

Arrays with in Structures

C permits the use of arrays as structure members.

```c
struct marks
    {
        int stno;
        float sub[3];
    };
struct marks  student [10];
```

here the member sub contains three elements sub[0], sub[1] and sub[2]. These elements can be accessed using appropriate subscripts.

Example

```c
student[1].sub[2];
```

would refer to the marks obtained in the third subject by the second student.

Structures with in Structures

Structures with in structures means nesting of structures.

```
        struct salary
          {
                char   name[10];
                char   dept[10];
                int       basic;
                int     da;
                int     hra;
                int     city_allowance;
          } employee;
```

This structure defines name, department, basic and three kinds of allowances together and declares them under a sub-structure as shown below.

```
struct employee                          struct  allow
{                                          {
char name[20];                                int da;
char dept[10];                                int hra;
struct allow_salary;                          int city;
};                                         }
struct   employee   emp;
```

The employee structure contains a member named salary which itself is a structure with three members. The members contained in the inner structure namely da, hra and city can be referred as

```
        emp.salary.da;
        emp.salary.hra;
        emp.salary.city;
```

typedef statement

The function of this statement is to redefine the name of an existing variable type.

For example, consider the following structure declaration

```
struct student
{
  int stno;
  char stname[10];
 int m1,m2,m3;
};
```

struct student s1;

This structure declaration can be made more easy to use when renamed using typedef as shown below:

```
struct student
{
  int stno;
  char stname[10];
 int m1,m2,m3;
};

typedef struct student stype;
 stype s1;
```

Structures and Functions

Any user-defined function can be performed on structure values by passing structure values as arguments to the function. This can be done in three ways:

(i)   Each member of a student can be passed individually as function arguments but this method becomes difficult when the structure contains more number of elements.

A Program to pass structures as function arguments

```
void display(int,float);
void main()
{
struct employee
{
int empid;
float salary;
```

```
};
struct employee e1={105,5000.5};
display(e1.empid,e1.salary);
}
void display(int id,float sal)
{
printf("empid=%d\nsalary=%f",id,sal);
}
```

    (ii)   A copy of entire structure can be passed from calling function to the called function. Here, the changes made in called function do not reflect in the calling function.

A Program to pass structures as function arguments

```
void display(struct employee);
void main()
{
struct employee
{
int empid;
float salary;
};
struct employee e1={105,5000.5};
display(e1);
}
void display(struct employee d)
{
printf("empid=%d\nsalary=%f",d.empid,d.salary)
;
}
```

    (iii)   The address location of the structure can be passed to the function. Here the changes made in the called function are reflected in the calling function.

A Program on passing location of structure to a function:
```
void display(struct book *);
void main()
{
struct book
{
```

```c
char name[10];
char author[10];
int pages;
};
struct book b1={"c&ds","dennis ",250};
display(&b1);
}
void display(struct book *b2)
{
printf("name=%s\nauthor=%s\npages=%d",(*b2).name,(*b2.author),
(*b2.pages));
}
```

Unions

Unions are same as structures in some aspects i.e., union is also a collection of different datatypes of elements stored under a single name but the major difference between union and structure is in terms of their storage. In structure, each member has its own storage location where as in a union all the members use the same location. All the members of the structure can be initialized at the same time but a union can handle only one member at a time. Since, the members of the union share the same memory.

Declaration of a union is same as that of structure declaration except that the keyword used is union.

Syntax:

```
        union tagname
        {
                datatype member 1;
                datatype member 2;
                :
                :
                :
                datatype member n;
        };
```

Example:

```
        union student
```

```
        {
                int rollno;
                float avg;
        }s1;
```

The storage is allocated for the member which occupies largest memory. Here, the union contains two datatypes int and float. Since, the largest is float and it occupies 4 bytes, s1 is allocated 4 bytes.

Representation:

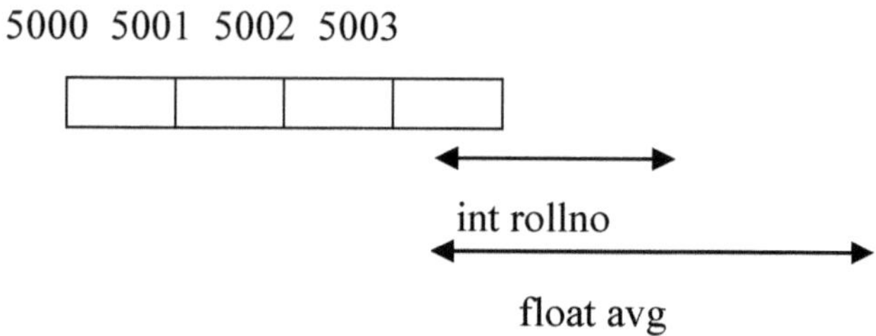

Program to illustrate difference between structure and union.

```
void main()
{
struct student
{
char name[10];
int rollno;
float avg;
}s1;
printf("no. of bytes for s1=%d",sizeof(s1));
 getch();
}
void main()
{
 union student
{
char name[10];
int rollno;
float avg;
}s1;
printf("no. of bytes for s1=%d",sizeof(s1));
 getch();
}
```

A Program to enter and print employee details using unions.

```c
void main()
{
union employee
{
char name[10];
int empid;
float salary;
}e1;
strcpy(e1.name,"Ajay");
printf("name=%s",e1.name);
e1.empid=50;
printf("empid=%d",e1.empid);
e1.salary=5000.5;
printf("salary=%f",e1.salary);
getch();
```

Bitfields

A bitfield is a set of adjacent bits whose size can be from 1 to 16 bits. Bit field provides exact amount of bits required to store values i.e., for example when an integer is declared, 2 bytes are allocated to store an integer which we may or may not completely utilize.

Therefore, to avoid wastage of memory, we mention the exact bit size. The name and size of bit fields are defined using a structure.

Syntax:
```c
Struct tagname
{
      datatype member 1:bit length;
      datatype member 2:bit length;
      :
      :
      datatype member n:bit length;
};
```

Here, the datatype can be either int or unsigned int or signed int.

Bit length specifies the number of bits used under that name. Here the colon(:) tells the compiler that bitfields are used in the structure. In a bitfield of lenght1 we can store the values 0,1. In a bitfield of lenght2 we can store the values 0,1,2,3. Similarly, in a bit field of lenght1 we can store the values 0,to 2^n-1.

A Program to implement bitfields.

```
#include<stdio.h>
#include<conio.h>
void main( )
{
struct employee
{
unsigned  empid:6;
unsigned age:5;
unsigned children:2;
}e1;
clrscr( );
e1.empid=59;
e1.age=29;
e1.children=2;
printf("details are\n");
printf("%u%u%u",e1.empid,e1.age,e1.children);
getch( );
}
```

Note:
1. *We cannot take address of a bitfield, hence pointers cannot be used to access bitfields.*
2. *scanf( ) statement cannot be used to read values in bitfields.*
3. *bitfields cannot be arrayed.*

5. Files

Objective

1. Provides knowledge of algorithms and flowcharts.
2. Teaches how to structure C programming.
3. Enhances understanding of the concepts of tokens, variables, data types, and their respective sizes.
4. Covers control statements in C programming.

In the dedicated exploration of this chapter, our focus centers on Files and their operations, delving into the fundamental aspects of file handling in programming. We navigate the intricacies of reading from and writing to files, understanding how these operations serve as vital mechanisms for data persistence and retrieval. From opening and closing files to performing essential read and write operations, we uncover the nuanced processes that enable programs to interact with external data sources. The chapter extends its gaze to file positioning, seeking, and manipulation, unravelling the techniques that empower programmers to navigate and modify data within files with precision. Throughout this exploration, Files emerge as dynamic entities, serving as conduits for data storage and exchange between programs and external sources. Join us in this chapter where the spotlight is cast upon the essential concepts and operations that govern the seamless interaction between programs and the realm of external data storage.

Files

Until now we have been using the functions such as scanf, printf to read and write data. These are console oriented I/O functions, which always use keyboard and screen as the target place. This works fine as long as the data is small. However, many real-life problems involve large volumes of data and in such situations, the console oriented I/O operations pose two major problems.

1. It becomes cumbersome and time consuming to handle large volumes of data through terminals.
2. The entire data is lost when either the program is terminated or the computer is turned off.

It is therefore necessary to have a more flexible approach where data can be stored on the disks and read whenever necessary, without destroying the data. This method employs the concept of files to store data.

A file is a place on the disk where a group of related data is stored. Like more other languages, C supports a number of functions that have the ability to perform basic file operations, which include

- Naming a file
- Opening a file
- Reading data from a file
- Writing data to a file
- Closing a file

Definition: A file is a set of records that can be accessed through a set of library functions.

Opening and Closing a file: A file has to be opened before beginning any operation on the file before opening a file we need to declare a pointer variable of type FILE where FILE is a predefined structure in stdio.h.

Defining and opening a file:

If we want to store data in a file in the secondary memory, we must specify certain things about the file, to the operating system. They include

1) File name
2) Data structure
3) Purpose

When we open a file , we must specify what we want to do with the file. For example, we may write data to the file or read the already existing data.

General format for declaring and opening a file:

```
FILE *fp;
fp=fopen("filename","mode");
```

The first statement declares the variable fp as a pointer to the data type FILE. FILE is a structure that is defined in the I/O library. The second statement opens the file named filename and assigns an identifier to the FILE type pointer fp. This contains all the information about the file and is subsequently used as a communication link between the system and the program.

Mode can be one of the following.

r -- open the file for reading only.
w --open the file for writing only
a --open the file for appending data to it

Note that both filename and mode are specified as strings. They should be enclosed in double quotation marks.

```
FILE   *fp1,*fp2;
   fp1=fopen("data.dat","w");
   fp2=fopen("stud.dat","r");
```

fopen( ):This is the function used to open a file.
Syntax:

```
       filepointer=fopen("filename","mode");
```

Where "filename" indicates the file to be open and mode indicates the purpose of opening a file.
Example:

```
            fp=fopen("pr1.txt","r");
```

Here pr1.txt is the file opened for reading purpose. When a file is opened in read mode, it does three things.
1.searches for the file to be opened.
2.if the file is found, it loads the file from disk into memory.
3.if the file is not found, it returns NULL.
4.it sets the pointer to the first character in the memory where the file has been done.

fclose( ): This function is used to close the file after the corresponding operation has been done.
        Syntax: fclose(file pointer);
        Example: fclose(fp);

File Opening Modes

The purpose of opening a file is mentioned as its mode. There are 6 modes in which we can open a file.

1. **"r"**(read mode): This mode is used to open an already existing file. If the file is found, it sets the   pointer to the first character in it. If the file is not found it returns NULL.

2. **"w"**(write mode): This mode is generally used to open a new file. If we try to open an existing file in write mode, all the previous data is lost. It returns NULL if unable to open the file.

3. **"a"**(append mode): This mode is used to add data to an already existing file. The data is added at the end of the file. If the file does not exists, a new file will be created with the given name. It returns NULL if unable to open the file.

4. **"w+"**(write and read mode): If an already existing file is opened in this mode, its contents are destroyed. Otherwise a new file is created. Writing new contents and reading them is possible in this mode. It returns NULL if unable to open the file.

5. **"r+"**(read and write mode): An already existing file is opened in this mode to read the contents of the file and write new contents .i.e., the old contents will be replaced with the new contents. It returns NULL if unable to open the file.

6. **"a+"**(append and read mode): An already existing file is opened in this mode to add contents at the end of the file. After appending, that contents can be read. It returns NULL if unable to open the file.

Standard I/O The operations on a file can be carried out by some standard IO functions. They are:

(i) **getc( ):** This function is used to read a single character from an opened file. After reading a character, the file pointer moves to the next character. It returns EOF if the end of the file is reached.

Syntax:

        Character variable=getc(file pointer);

Example:

        Ch=getc(fp);

(ii) **putc( ):** This function is used to write a single character into a file.

Syntax:
                putc(character variable, file pointer);
        Example:
                putc(ch, fp);

(iii)   **fgets( ):** This function is used to read a string from a file.
        Syntax:
                fgets(string variable, length, file pointer);
        Example:
                fgets(s,10,fp);
Here s indicates the address location where the string is stored,
second argument indicates maximum length of the string and
third argument indicates file pointer.

(iv)   **fputs( ):** This function is used to write a string into a file.
        Syntax:
                fputs(string variable, file pointer);
        Example:
                fputs(s, fp);

(v)   **getw( ):** This function can be used to read an integer value
from a file.
        Syntax:
                integer variable=getw(file pointer);
        Example:
                i=getw(fp);

(vi)   **putw( ):** This function is used to write an integer into a file.
        Syntax:
                putw(integer variable, file pointer);
        Example:
                putw(i, fp);

A Program to create a new file and enter contents to it.

```c
#include<stdio.h>
#include<conio.h>
void main( )
{
FILE *fp;
Char ch;
```

```c
clrscr( );
fp=fopen("file1.txt","w");
while((ch=getchar( ))!=EOF)
{
        putc(ch,fp);
          }
          fclose(fp);
          getch( );
}
```

A Program to read the contents of an existing file and display them.

```c
#include<stdio.h>
#include<conio.h>
#include<stdlib.h>
void main( )
{
FILE *fp;
Char ch;
clrscr( );
fp=fopen("file1.txt","r");
if(fp==NULL)
{
printf("cannot open the file");
exit(0);
}
while((ch=getchar( ))!=EOF)
{
        putchar(ch);
          }
          fclose(fp);
          getch( );
}
```

A Program to copy contents of one file to another.

```c
#include<stdio.h>
#include<conio.h>
void main( )
{
FILE *fs,*ft;
char ch;
```

```c
fs=fopen("file1.txt","r");
if(fs==NULL)
{
printf("cannot open file");
exit(0);
            }
ft=fopen("file2.txt","w");
if(ft==NULL)
{
printf("cannot open file");
exit(0);
            }
            while((ch=getc(fs))!=EOF)
            {
                    putc(ch, ft);
            }
            fclose(ft);
            printf(" the copied contents are
\n");
            ft=fopen("file2.txt", "r");
            while((ch=getc(ft))!=EOF)
            {
putchar(ch);
                    }
                fclose(fs);
                fclose(ft);
                getch( );
            }
```

A Program to separate even and odd numbers into 2 files.

```c
#include<stdio.h>
#include<conio.h>
void main( )
{
        FILE *fp1,*fp2,*fp3;
        int i, n, x;
   clrscr( );
        fp1=fopen("file1.txt","w");
        if(fp1==NULL)
        {
                printf("file cannot be opened");
```

```c
            exit(0);
      }
      printf("enter number of values");
      scanf("%d",&n);
      printf("enter values\n");
      for(i=1;i<=n;i++)
      {
            scanf("%d",&x);
            putw(x,fp1);
      }
      fclose(fp1);
      fp1=fopen("file1.txt","r");
      fp2=fopen("even.txt","w");
      fp3=fopen("odd.txt","w");
      for(i=1;i<=n;i++)
      {
            x=getw(fp1);
            if(x%2==0)
            putw(x,fp2);
            else
            putw(x,fp3);
      }
      fclose(fp1);
      fclose(fp2);
      fclose(fp3);
      fp2=fopen("even.txt","r");
      fp3=fopen("odd.txt","r");
      printf("contents of even file are\n");
      while((x=getw(fp2)!=EOF)
      {
            printf("%d ",x);
   }
      printf("contents of odd file are\n");
      while((x=getw(fp3)!=EOF)
      {
            printf("%d ",x);
   }
      fclose(fp2);
      fclose(fp3);
      getch( );
   }
```

A Program to enter and print the contents of a file by using fgets( ) and fputs( ) functions.

```c
#include<stdio.h>
#include<conio.h>
#include<stdlib.h>
void main ( )
{
FILE *fp;
char s[10];
clrscr( );
fp=fopen("file1.txt","w");
if(fp==NULL)
{
printf("cannot open the file");
exit(0);
}
while(strlen(gets(s))>0)
{
fputs(s,fp);
fputs("\n",fp);
}
fclose(fp);
fp=fopen("file1.txt","r");

while(fgets(s,9,fp)!=NULL)
{
        puts(s);
        printf("\n");
          }
          fclose(fp);
          getch( );
}
```

Formatted I/O

The formatted reading and writing of characters, strings, integers, floating point numbers, we had functions namely fscanf( ) and fprintf( ).

fscanf( ):This function is used to read any type of information from a file.

Syntax:

```
fscanf(filepointer,"control strings", &variables);
```

Example:

```
fscanf(fp,"%c%d%f",&a,&b,&c);
```

fprintf( ): This function is used to write different data types of information into a file.

Syntax:

```
fprintf("filepointer,"control strings", &variables);
```

Example: `fprintf(fp,"%c%d%f",a,b,c);`

A Program to enter details of a student into a file and display them.

```
#include<stdio.h>
#include<conio.h>
void main( )
{
struct student
{
char name[10];
int rollno;
char grade;
}s[2];
FILE *fp;
int i;
fp=fopen("student.txt","w+");
for(i=0;i<2;i++)
{
printf("enter details of student %d",i+1);
scanf("%s%d",s[i].name,&s[i].rollno);
fflush(stdin);
scanf("%c",&s[i].grade);
fprintf(fp,"%s%d%c",s[i].name,s[i].rollno,s[i]
.grade);
}
```

```
for(i=0;i<2;i++)
{
fscanf(fp,"%s%d%c",s[i].name,&s[i].rollno,&s[i
].grade);
printf("details are\n");
printf("%s%d%c",s[i].name,s[i].rollno,s[i].gra
de);
}
fclose(fp);
}
```

ftell( ): This function indicates the current position in the file.
Syntax:variable=ftell(file pointer);

fseek( ): This function is used to move to a desired position in a file.
Syntax:fseek(filepointer,offset,position);

File pointer is the pointer through which the file has been opened.
offset indicates the number of bytes that are to be moved.
Position can take three values
0-> starting of the file.
1->current position of the file.
2->ending of the file.
These three positions can also be indicated through
SEEK_SET,SEEK_CUR,SEEK_END respectively.
Example: fseek(fp,2L,0);
It indicates the filepointer to be moved 2 bytes from the starting of
the file.
Example: fseek(fp,-3L,1);
It indicates the filepointer to be moved 3 bytes backward from the
current position.
Example: fseek(fp,-5L,2);
It indicates the filepointer to be moved 5 bytes backward from the
ending of the file.

Rewind( ): This function is used to go to the starting of the file at any
time.
Syntax: rewind(filepointer);
Example: rewind(fp);

A Program using the function ftell( )

```c
#include<stdio.h>
#include<conio.h>
#include<stdlib.h>
void main( )
{
        FILE *fp;
        char ch;
        long int m,n;
        clrscr( );
        fp=fopen("file1.txt","w");
        if(fp==NULL)
        {
                printf("cannot open the file");
                exit(0);
        }
        m=ftell(fp);
        printf("starting position=%ld",m);
        while((ch=getc(fp))!=EOF)
        {
                printf("%c",ch);
        }
        n=ftell(fp);
        printf("ending position=%ld",n);
        fclose(fp);
        getch( );
}
```

Binary Files

There are two types of files. (i) text files (i) binary files.
The major differences between text files and binary files are
   (i)   The new line character is stored as two characters in text
            file where as it is stored as single character in a binary
            file.
   (ii)   End of file is indicated with Ctrl+Z combination in a text
            file where as no such indication is srquired in binary files.
   (iii)   All the data is treated as individual characters and each
            character occupies one byte in text files. In binary files,
            the data is treated according to the corresponding data
            type.

A Program using the functions fread( ) and fwrite( ):

```c
#include<stdio.h>
#include<conio.h>
void main( )
{
struct employee
{
char name[10];
int age;
float salary;
}e;
FILE *fp;
fp=fopen("employee.dat","wb+");
printf("enter details ");
scanf("%s%d%f",e.name,&e.age,&e.salary);
fwrite(&e,sizeof(e),1,fp);
rewind(fp);
printf("details are\n");
while((fread(&e,sizeof(e),1,fp)==1)
printf("%s%d%f",e.name,e.age,e.salary);
fclose(fp);
getch( );
}
```

Error Handling

An operation on a file may not be successful sometimes. The type of errors that may occur are:

- Trying to read beyond end of the file
- Device overflow
- Trying to use a file that has not been opened.
- Opening a file with an invalid name.
- Trying to perform an operation while the file is opened for other mode.

Ferror( );-   This function is used to report any sort of these errors occurred during operation on a file. It returns 1 if an error occurs and otherwise 0.

Syntax:ferror(filepointer);
Feof( ): This function can be used to check whether the end of the file is reached or not.It returns a non-zero value if end of file is reached and a zero value otherwise.
Syntax:feof(filepointer);

A Program using functions ferror( ) and feof( ):

```
#include<stdio.h>
#include<conio.h>
void main( )
{
     FILE *fp;
     clrscr( );
     fp=fopen("file1.txt","w");
     while(!(feof(fp)))
     {
         ch=getc(fp);
         if(ferror(fp)
         {
                   printf("error");
                   exit(0);
         }
         putchar(ch);
     }
     fclose(fp);
     getch( );
}
```

6. Searching and Sorting

Objective

1. Provides you the knowledge on data structures
2. Enhance the understanding the concepts of Stack, Queues and LinkedList
3. Covers the operations of various concepts

In the realms of this chapter, our exploration centers on the critical topics of searching and sorting algorithms. Delving into the art of searching, we unravel the methods and strategies employed to efficiently locate specific elements within datasets, whether through linear searches for simplicity or binary searches for enhanced speed in ordered lists. The narrative seamlessly transitions to sorting, where we explore the various algorithms designed to arrange data systematically. From the straightforward bubble sort to the sophisticated quicksort and mergesort, we delve into the intricacies of organizing information in a manner that optimizes retrieval and enhances the overall efficiency of programs. As we navigate through the landscapes of searching and sorting, these fundamental algorithms emerge as the keystones of effective data manipulation, empowering programmers to streamline information retrieval and maintain organized datasets. Join us in this chapter, where the discussions on searching and sorting unfold, shaping the foundations of algorithmic efficiency in the realm of programming.

Searching

Searching is the technique of finding accurate location of an element in the given set of elements. If the element is found in the set of elements it is said to be a successful search. Otherwise an unsuccessful search.

Searching methods are of two types:
(i)Linear (Sequential)Search
(ii)Binary Search

Linear Search:

Linear search is a method of searching an element in a list in sequence i.e., starting from the first element to the last element, the entire list is searched for the element. This method can be applied on sorted or unsorted set of elements.

Example:

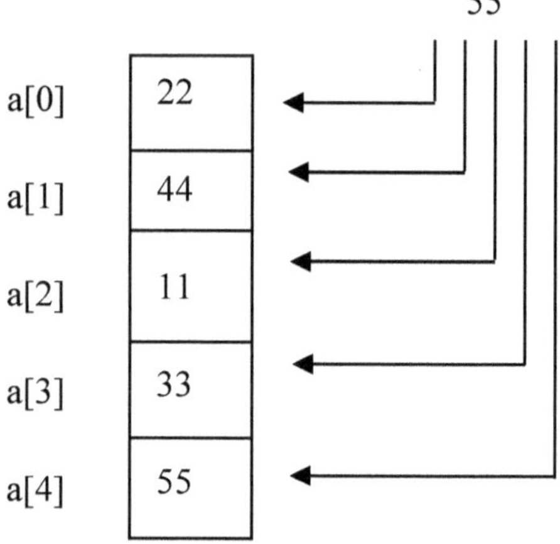

In the above example, element is found in the last position.
Time complexity of best case linear search is O(1).
Time complexity of worst case linear search is O(n), where n is the number of elements in the list.
Advantage: It is easier to implement than other searching elements.
Disadvantage: It requires more number of comparisons.

A program to implement linear search.

```c
#include<stdio.h>
#include<conio.h>
void main( )
{
int a[10],i,n,search;
printf("Enter no of elements \n");
scanf("%d",&n);
printf("Enter elements \n");
for(i=0;i<n;i++)
scanf("%d",&a[i]);
printf("Enter element to be searched\n");
scanf("%d",&search);
for(i=0;i<n;i++)
{
if(a[i]==search)
    {
printf(" %d is found at %d
position",search,i+1);
exit();
}
}
printf("element %d is not found", search);
getch( );
}
```

Binary Search

In this method of searching, the entire list is made into two halves. Hence it creates two parts, it is known as binary search. But this method cannot be implemented on an unsorted list. To apply this method, the list has to be sorted either in ascending or descending order. So, after sorting first the search element is compared with mid element of the list. If it is before the middle element, it is searched in the first half. Otherwise in the second half.

Example:

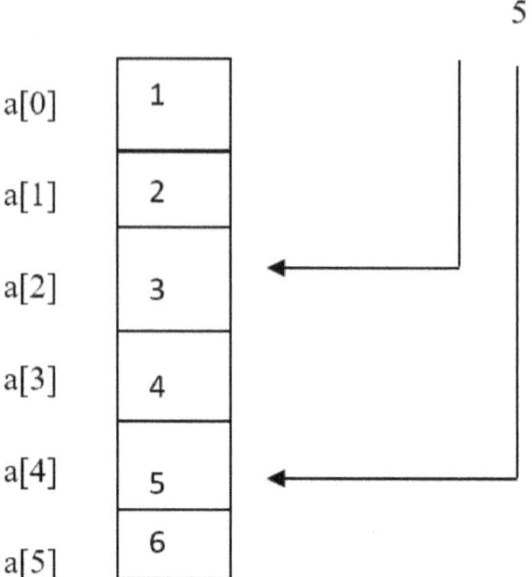

In the above example of list 1,2,3,4,5,6 the search element is 5 and it falls under second half of the list. So, the second half of the list is searched for 5.

The time complexity for the best case binary search is O(1). The time complexity of worst-case binary search is O($\log_2 n$).

Advantage: It requires less number of comparisons than that of the linear search.

Disadvantages:1. It works on sorted data only.

2. It is hard to implement than that of linear search.

A program to implement binary search.

```c
int bin_search(int a[ ], int n, int ele);

void main( )
{
int a[10],i,n,ele,pos;
printf("enter the size of an array \n");
scanf("%d",&n);
printf("enter elements :\n");
for(i=0;i<n;i++)
scanf("%d",&a[i]);
printf("Enter element to be searched\n");
```

```c
scanf("%d",&ele);
pos=bin-search(a,n,ele);
if(pos>=0)
{
printf("Elements %d is found at %d position",
ele,pos+1);
exit(0);
}
else
printf("Element is not found");
getch();
}
int bin-search(int a[ ],int n,int ele)
{
int low,high,mid;
low=0;
high=n-1;
while(low<=high)
{
mid=(low+high)/2;
if(ele==a[mid])
high=mid-1;
else
low=mid+1;
}
return(-1);
}
```

Sorting

Sorting is a process in which the elements are arranged in ascending or descending order.

Bubble Sort

This is the simplest sorting technique when compared to other sorting techniques.

Process:

1. If we consider an array A[n] elements, first the two elements of the array A[0] and A[1] are compared. If A[1]>A[0], then the two values are interchanged.

2.Then compare A[1] and A[2].If A[2]>A[1], interchange those values.

3.continue this process till the last two elements are compared and interchanged.

4.Repeat the above steps for (n-1) passes.

After completion of 1st pas, the largest element is placed in nth position. After second pass, the second largest is placed in (n-1)th position .Similarly after)n-1) passes, all the n elements will get sorted.

Tracing:

Let the array be a[5]={55,45,35,25,15}

I pass:

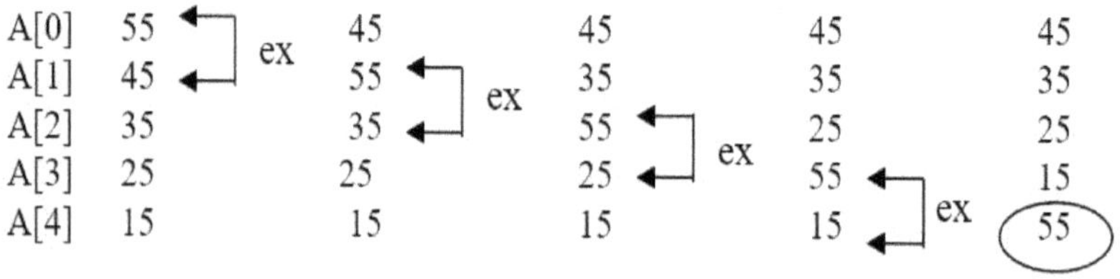

A[0]	55		45		45		45	45
A[1]	45	ex	55		35		35	35
A[2]	35		35	ex	55		25	25
A[3]	25		25		25	ex	55	15
A[4]	15		15		15		15	ex (55)

II pass:

A[0]	55	ex	45		45		45	45
A[1]	45		55	ex	35		35	35
A[2]	35		35		55	ex	25	25
A[3]	25		25		25		55	15
A[4]	15		15		15		15	ex (55)

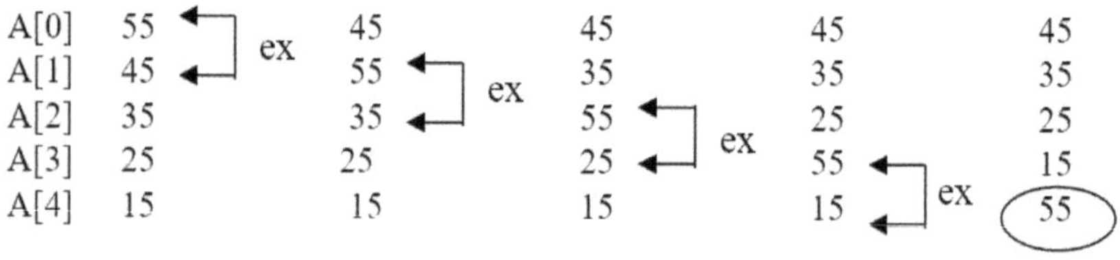

III pass:

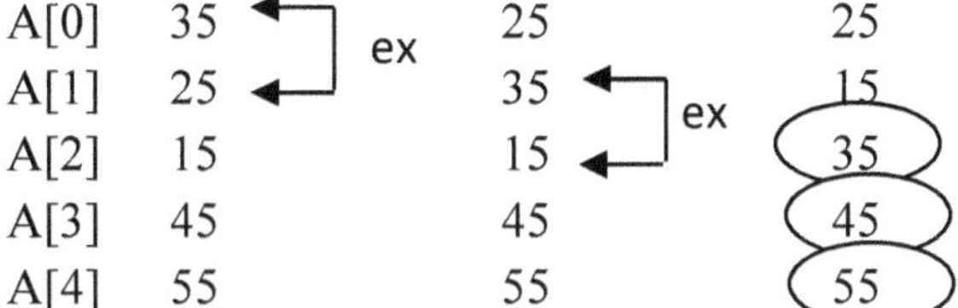

IV pass:

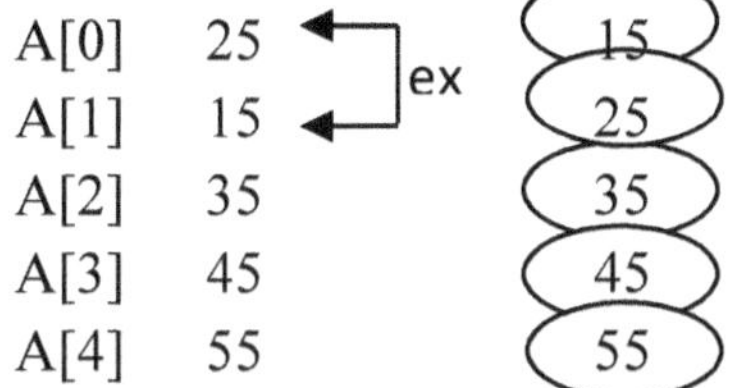

A program to implement Bubble sort.

```c
#include<stdio.h>
#include<conio.h>
void main( )
{
int a[10],i,j,n,temp;
printf("enter the size of an array \n");
scanf("%d",&n);
printf("enter elements :\n");
for(i=0;i<n;i++)
scanf("%d",&a[i]);
for(i=0;i<n;i++)
{
for(j=0;j<n-1;j++)
{
if(a[j]>a[j+1])
{
temp=a[j];
a[j]=a[j+1];
a[j+1]=temp;
}
}
```

```
                    }
                                printf("Sorted order
          is");

                                for(i=0;i<n;i++)
                                printf("%d\n",a[i]);
                                getch( );

          }
```

Selection Sort

Process:

1. In the first step, the smallest element is searched in the list once the smallest element is found ,it is exchanged with the element in the first position.

2.In the next step, the second smallest element is searched and it is interchanged with the element

in the second position.

3.This process is repeated until all the elements are sorted.

4.Thus it requires a maximum of (n-1) passes to completer the sorting.

Tracing:

Let the array be a[5]={30,40,4,5,10}

I pass:

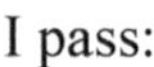

```
     A[0]    30             4
     A[1]    40      ex     40
     A[2]    4              30
     A[3]    5              5
     A[4]    10             10
```

II pass:

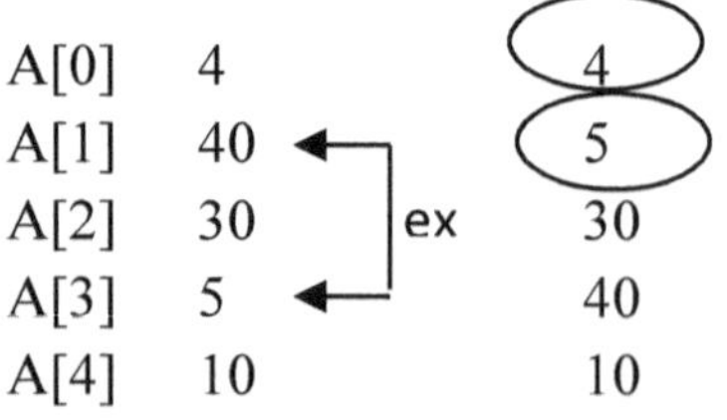

```
     A[0]    4              4
     A[1]    40             5
     A[2]    30      ex     30
     A[3]    5              40
     A[4]    10             10
```

III pass:

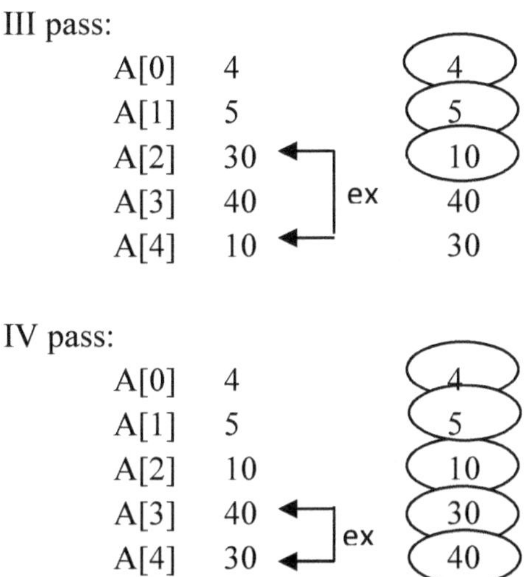

IV pass:

A program to implement Selection sort.

```c
#include<stdio.h>
#include<conio.h>
void sel_sort(int x[ ], int n);
void main( )
{
int x[10],i,j,n;
printf("Enter the size of an array \n");

scanf("%d",&n);
printf("Enter elements :\n");
for(i=0;i<n;i++)
scanf("%d",&x[i]);
sel_sort(x,n);
printf("Sorted order is \n");
for(i=0;i<n;i++)
printf("%d  ",x[i]);
getch( );
}
void sel_sort(int x[ ], int n)
```

```
{
        int i,j,index,small;
        for(i=0;i<n;i++)
        {
                small=x[i];
                index=i;
                for(j=i+1;j<n;j++)
                {
                        if(x[j]<small)
                        {
                                small=x[j];
                                index=j;
                        }
                }
                x[index]=x[i];
                x[i]=small;
        }
}
```

Merge Sort

In this sorting technique, two separate sorted arrays are taken and the process continues as follows:

1. The first element of the first array is compared with the first element of the second array. The smallest of the two is placed in the third array.
2. The next two elements of the two sorted arrays are compared and the smallest is stored in the third array.
3. This process continues until any of the two arrays reaches its end.
4. The remaining elements of the other array are copied to the third array. Thus the third array contains the sorted order with merging the two given arrays.

A program to implement merge sort.

```c
#include<stdio.h>
#include<conio.h>
void merge_sort(int a[ ],int b[ ],int c[ ],
int n1, int n2,int *n);
void main( )
    {
    int a[10],b[10],c[20],n1,n2,n,i;
          clrscr( );
    printf("Enter size of first array:");
    scanf("%d",&n1);
    printf("Enter elements of first array in
        sorted order \n");
    for(i=0;i<n;i++)
    scanf("%d",&a[i]);
    printf("Enter size of second array:");
    scanf("%d",&n2);
    printf("Enter elements of second array in
        sorted order \n");
    for(i=0;i<n2;i++)
    scanf("%d",&b[i]);
    merge_sort(a,b,c,n1,n2,&n);
    printf("After sorting\n");
    for(i=0;i<n;i++)
    printf("%d  ",c[i]);
    for(i=0;i<n;i++)
    printf("%d  ",c[i]);
    getch( );
    }
    void merge_sort(int a[],int b[],int c[],
    int n1, int n2,int *n)
    {
    int i=0;j=0;k=0;
    while((i<n1)&&(j<n2))
    {
    if(a[i]<b[j])
```

```
{
c[k]=a[i];
i++;
}
else
{
c[k]=b[j];
j++;
}
k++;
}
while(i<n1)
{
c[k]=a[i];
i++;
K++;
}
while(j<n2)
{
c[k]=b[j];
j++;
k++;
}
*n=k;
}
```

Example: Let a[2]={56,78} and b[3]={45,67,89}
The resultant array after merge sort will be
C[5]={45,56,67,78,89}

The efficiency of merge sort is given by O(nlogn).

Insertion Sort

This technique works well when the number of elements is less.
Process:

1. The first element of the array is assumed to be sorted.
2. The second element is compared with the first element and it is inserted before or after the first element according to the order. Thus the first two elements are sorted.
3. The third element is compared with first two elements and it is inserted either before first and second elements or between first and second elements or after first and second elements. Thus the first three elements are sorted.
4. Similarly, the n elements will be sorted in (n-1)passes.

Tracing:

Let the array be a[5]={50,40,30,20,10}

I pass:

II pass:

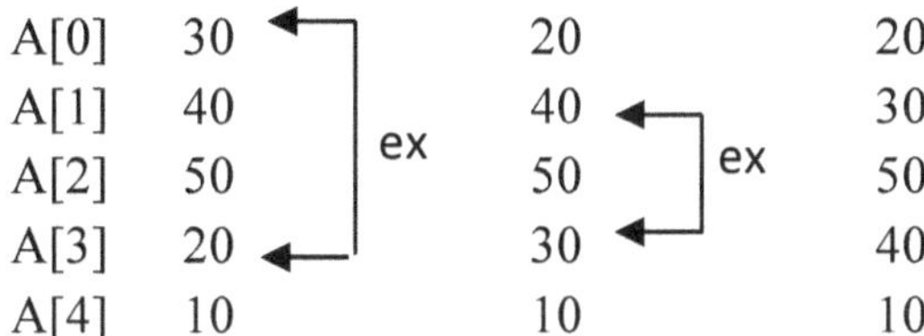

III pass:

IV pass:

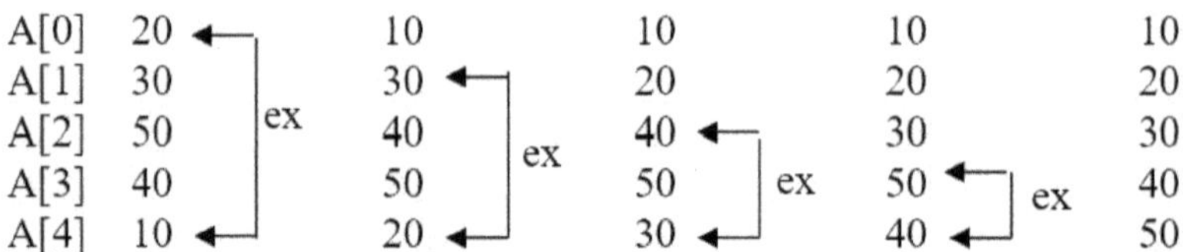

Time complexity of insertion sort is given by $O(n^2)$.

A program to implement Insertion sort.

```c
#include<stdio.h>
#include<conio.h>
void main( )
{
int a[10],i,j,n,small;
clrscr( );
printf("enter the size of an array \n");
scanf("%d",&n);
printf("enter elements :\n");
for(i=0;i<n;i++)
scanf("%d",&a[i]);
for(i=0;i<n;i++)
{
    small=a[i];
      j=i;
      while((j>0)&&a[j-i]>small)
      {
      a[j]=a[j-i];
      j--;
                }
      a[j]=small;
}

      printf("Sorted order is\n");
      for(i=0;i<n;i++)
      printf("%d  ",a[i]);
}
```

Quick Sort

This sorting technique is efficient when the number of elements is large.

Process:

1. In this method, a key value (or pivot) is selected (which is by default the first element) and the list is made into two parts such that all the elements on the left side of the key are less than the key element and all the elements on the right side are greater than the key value. Then interchanging these two values.

2. This can be achieved when we scan the list from the right until we get an element that is less than key value and scan from left until we get the element greater than the key value. Then interchange those two values.

3. When the left and right searching's are crossed then interchange the element in the right position with the key value.

I pass:

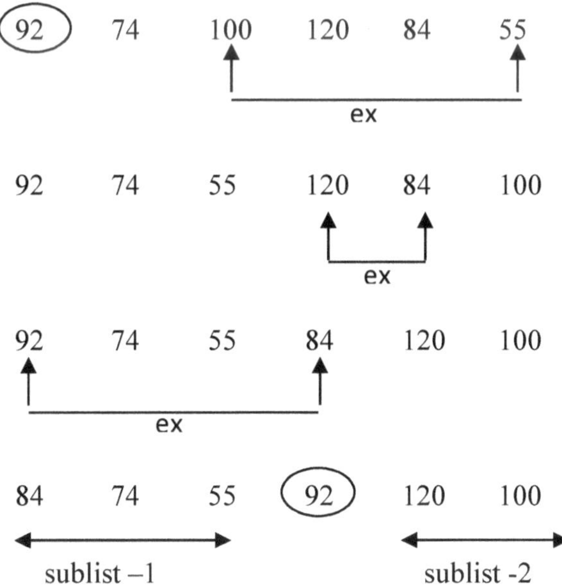

II pass:

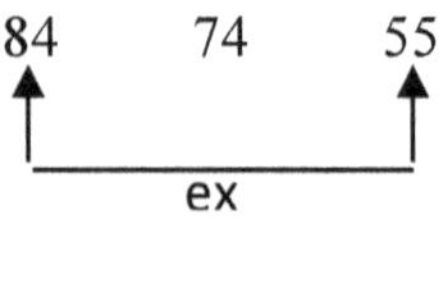

84   74   55

55   74   84

III pass:

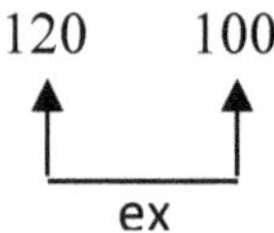

100   120

Thus the sorted list is : 55   74   84   92   100   120

Efficiency of Quick Sort:

Efficiency of quick sort can be calculated in two cases.

(i)   In this case, we take two assumptions is

The key element divides the given list into exactly two halves.

Number of elements in the list is the power of 2.

i.e., if n elements are there, $n=2^y$

$$y=\log_2 n$$

for the first pass, it takes n comparisons for n elements. In the second pass, it takes n/2 comparisons for each half and so on. Thus the efficiency of quick sort in best case can be calculated as

$O(n)+O(n)+O(n)+\ldots\ldots\ldots+y$ terms.

$=O(n*y)$

$=O(n*\log_2 n)$

$=O(n\log n)$.

(ii)   In this case, the assumption is

The key element divide4s the elements such that all the elements are on the same side of the key. Thus the efficiency of quick sort in worst case is given by

$$(n-1)+(n-2)+(n-3)+\ldots\ldots+1$$
$$=(n-1)*n/2$$
$$=(n^2-n)/2$$
$$=\tfrac{1}{2}(n^2-n)$$

By neglecting the constant ½, and the term n,
$=O(n^2)$.

A program to implement Quick sort.

```c
#include<stdio.h>
#include<conio.h>
int partition(int m,int n);
void quick_sort(int p,int q);
int a[10];
void main( )
{
int i,size,p=0,q;
printf("Enter size of array\n");
scanf("%d",&size);
q=size-1;
printf("Enter elements:");
for(i=0;i,size;i++)
scanf("%d",&a[i]);
quick_sort(p,q);
printf("After sorting ");
for(i=0;i,size;i++)
scanf("%d  ",&a[i]);
getch( );
}
void quick_sort(int p,int q)
{
int j;
if(p<q)
{
j=partition(p,q+1);
quick_sort(p,j-1);
quick_sort(j+1,q);
}
}
int(partition(int m,int n)
```

```c
{
int key,l,r,temp;
key=a[m];
l=m;
r=n;
do
{
do
{
l++;
}
while(a[l]<key);
do
{
r--;
}
while(a[r]>key);
if(l<r)
{
temp=a[l];
a[l]=a[r];
a[r]=temp;
}
}
while(l<r);
a[m]=a[r];
a[r]=key;
return( r);
}
```

7. Data Structures

Objective

1. Provides you the knowledge on data structures
2. Enhance the understanding the concepts of Stack, Queues and LinkedList
3. able to implement the various operations is data structures

Within the pages of this chapter, a profound exploration unfolds, delving into the fundamental concepts of Data Structures. Serving as the bedrock of efficient computing, Data Structures provide a systematic framework for organizing and manipulating data, a critical foundation for algorithmic design and software development. Our journey commences with Stacks, where the Last-In-First-Out (LIFO) dynamics govern their architecture. Stacks, resembling a vertical arrangement of elements, emerge as indispensable tools for scenarios demanding orderly data access, from managing function calls to evaluating mathematical expressions. The narrative seamlessly transitions to Queues, embodying the First-In-First-Out (FIFO) order, and playing a pivotal role in maintaining the sequence of operations, be it task scheduling or breadth-first tree traversal. As the exploration deepens, we navigate the dynamic landscape of Linked Lists, where pointers interconnect nodes, providing unbounded flexibility and efficiency in insertion and deletion operations. In unison, Stacks, Queues, and Linked Lists form a triad of dynamic structures, each contributing to the symphony of structured data organization and manipulation. This chapter serves as a beacon, illuminating the principles that underlie these fundamental Data Structures, empowering readers with the knowledge to architect algorithms and software solutions that embody efficiency, scalability, and adaptability.

Introduction To Data Structures:

Definition: A Data structure is an arrangement of data in an organized way in computer's memory.

Data structures can be classified into two types:
    (i) Linear data structures: Data structures using sequential allocation are called linear data structures.
    Example: arrays, stacks, queues, linked lists.

    (ii) Non-linear data structures: Data structures using linked allocation are called non-linear data structures.
    Example: trees, graphs.

Stacks

A stack is an ordered list in which all the insertion and deletion operations are made at one end. This end is represented as top of the stack. A stack works on the principle Last In First Out(LIFO). i.e., the last element inserted into the stack willl be the first one to be deleted.

Representation:

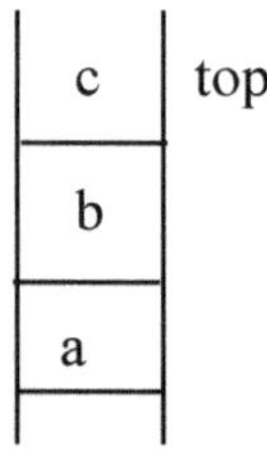

Here, the first element that can be deleted is the topmost element. i.e., c. In a stack, the operations insertion and deletion are possible. Insertion of an element into a stack is called PUSH operation and deletion of an element from a stack is called POP operation.

Stack overflow: It is the condition where the stack is full and no more elements can be inserted into the stack.
Stack underflow: It is the condition where the stack is empty and no elements can be deleted from the stack.

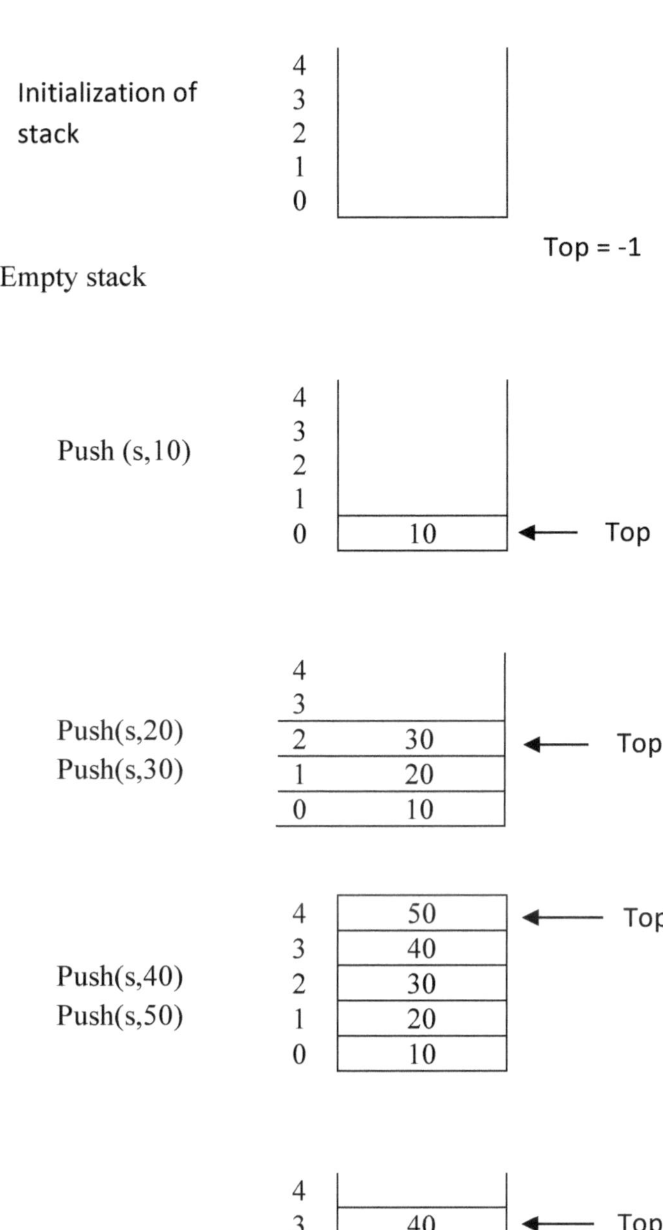
Initialization of stack
4
3
2
1
0
Top = -1
Empty stack
Push (s,10)
4
3
2
1
0
10
Top
Push(s,20)
Push(s,30)
4
3
2
30
1
20
0
10
Top
Push(s,40)
Push(s,50)
4
50
3
40
2
30
1
20
0
10
Top
X = pop(s)
4
3
40
2
30
20
0
10
Top

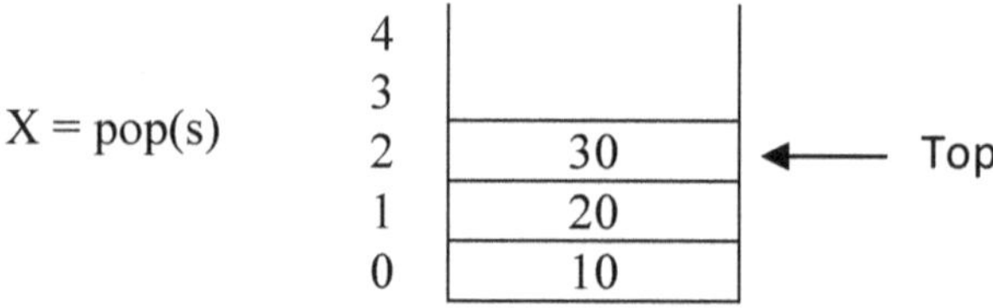

A motion picture of stack

At each point, the top element is removed, since a deletion can be made at only from the top. The most important thing is that the last element inserted into the stack is the first element deleted. For this reason a stack is some times called as LIFO (Last In First Out) list.

A helpful analogy is to think of a stack of trays or of plates sitting on a counter in a busy cafeteria. Though out the lunch hour customers take trays off the top of the stack, and the employees place returned trays back on top of the stack. The tray most recently put on the stack is the first one taken off. The bottom tray is the first one put on, and the last one to be used.

A Program to implement stack using arrays.

```
#define max 20
void push(int);
int pop();
void display();
int stack[max],top=-1;
void main()
{
  int ch,ele;
  printf("1.Push\n2.Pop\n3.Display");
  do
    {
      printf("Enter ur choice");
      scanf("%d",&ch);
      switch(ch)
        {
                case 1: printf("Enter element to be inserted");
                scanf("%d",&ele);
```

```c
                                        push(ele);
                                        break;
                            case 2: ele=pop();
                                    if(ele!=-1)
                                printf("Deleted element is %d",ele);
                                        break;
                            case 3: display();
                                        break;
    }
  }while(ch>=1&&ch<=3);
getch();
}
void push(int ele)
        {
 if(top>=max-1)
 printf("stack is full");
else
  {
top++;

stack[top]=ele;
        }
int pop()
{
 int ele;
 if(top==-1)
            {
printf("Stack is empty");
return(-1);
            }
 else
  {
ele=stack[top];
top--;
return(ele);
            }
        }
void display()
{
 if(top==-1)
 printf("Stack is empty");
 else
```

```
{
for(i=0;i<=top;i++)
printf("%d" stack[i]);
        }
    }
```

Queue

Queue is an ordered linear data structure in which elements are appended at one end and deleted at the other end. The end at which elements can be appended is called rear end and the end at which elements can be deleted is called front end. The principle involved in queue is First In First Out (FIFO) .i.e., the element first inserted can be deleted first.

Representation:

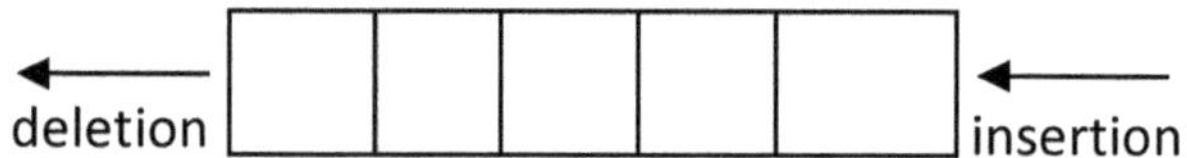

Examples

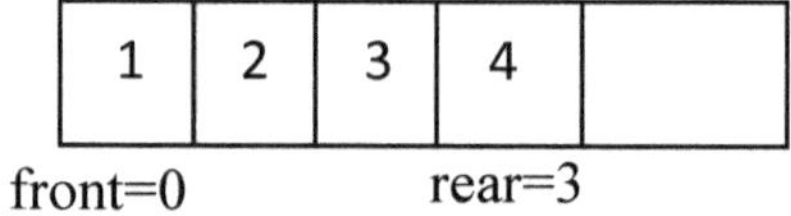

Insertion:

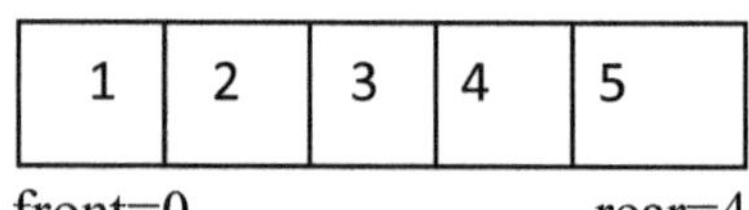

Deletion:

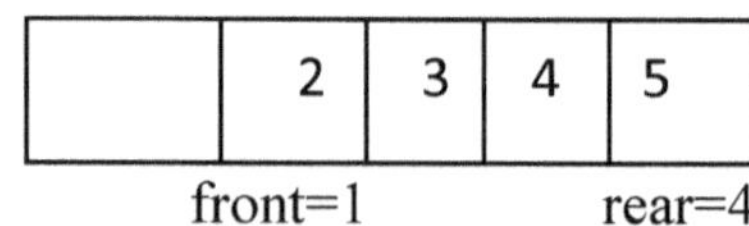

A Queue is an ordered collection of items from which items may be deleted at one end called the front of the Queue and into which items may be inserted at the other end called the rear of the queue.

Empty Q						Front = 0
	0	1	2	3	4	Rear = -1

Insert(Q,10)	10					Front = 0
	0	1	2	3	4	Rear = 0

Insert(Q,20)	10	20				Front = 0
	0	1	2	3	4	Rear = 1

Insert(Q,30) Insert(Q,40) Insert(Q,50)	10	20	30	40	50	Front = 0
	0	1	2	3	4	Rear = 4

x = delete(q)		20	30	40	50	Front = 1
	0	1	2	3	4	Rear = 4

x = delete(q)			30	40	50	Front = 2
	0	1	2	3	4	Rear = 4

The first element inserted into the queue is the first element to be removed. For this reason a queue is some times called a FIFO (First In First Out) list.

In ordinary english a queue is defined as a waiting line, like a line of people waiting to purchase tickets, where the first person in the queue is the First person served.

There are 3 primitive operations that can be applied to a queue.
INSERT

DELETE
EMPTY

The operation insert inserts an element at the rear of the queue.

The operation delete deletes the front element from the queue.
The operation empty returns 1 or 0 (true or false) depending on whether or not the queue contains any elements.

The condition where the queue is empty is called queue underflow and the condition where the queue is full is called queue overflow.

A Program to implement queue using arrays.

```c
#define max 20
void enqueue(int);
int dequeue();
void display();
int queue[max],f=0,r=-1;
void main()
{
    int ele, ch;
    do
      {
          printf("1.Enqueue\n 2.Dequeue \n3.Display\n");
      printf("Enter ur choice");
scanf("%d", &ch);
switch(ch)
{
    case 1: printf("Enter element to be inserted");
            scanf("%d",&ele);
            enqueue(ele);
             break;
    case 2: ele=dequeue();
         if(ele!=-1)
         printf("Deleted element is %d",ele);
         break;
    case 3: display();
         break;
        }
  }
              while(ch>=1&&ch<=3);
```

```c
        }
    void enqueue(int ele)
        {
                r++;
                 if(r>=max-1)
                printf("queue is full");
                else
                    {
        queue[r]=ele;
                    }
        }
    int dequeue()
        {
                int ele;
                if(f>r)
                    {
                        printf("queue is empty");
                    }

                else
                    {
                        ele=queue[f];
                        f++;
                        return(ele);
                    }
        }
    void display()
        {
                int i;
                if(f>r)
                    {
                        printf("queue is empty");
                    }
                else
                    {
                        for(i=f;i<=r;i++)
                        printf("%d ",queue[i]);
                    }
        }
```

Infix, Prefix and Postfix

A given arithmetic expression can be expressed in three ways:
Infix, Prefix and Postfix.

Infix: I f the operator is present between the operands, it is known as infix expression.
Example: a+b,a*(b+c), a/b%c etc.
Prefix: If the operator precedes the operands, it is known as prefix expression.
Example:+ab, /*abc,+-xyz etc.
Postfix: If the operator succeeds the operands, it is known as postfix expression.
Example:ab+,abc+*,ab/c% etc.

Conversion of Infix to Postfix

 A given infix expression can be converted to postfix by using the following algorithm.

Algorithm:
1. Initialize the stack to be empty and scan the given expression from left to right.
2. If an operand is found, append it to the output.
3. If an operator is found, if the stack is empty or the operator has higher priority than the operator on the top of the stack, push it on to the stack.
4. If the operator has lower priority or equal priority than the operator on the top of the stack, pop the operator from the top of the stack and append it to the output.
5. If left parenthesis is found, push it on to the stack.
6. If right parenthesis is found, pop the operators from the stack until left parenthesis is found.
7. Repeat the steps 2,3,4,5 and 6 until the right most end is reached. Pop the remaining operators from the stack and append to the output.

Example: a*(b+c)

Input	output	stack
A	a	----
*	a	*
(	a	*(

b	ab	*(
+	ab	*(+
c	abc	*(+
)	abc+	*
	abc+*	

Thus, the equivalent postfix expression is abc+*

Example: Converting A+B*C into postfix expression.

S.No.	Symb	Postfix String	Opstk
1	A	A	
2	+	A	+
3	B	AB	+
4	*	AB	+ *
5	C	ABC	+ *
6		ABC *	
7		ABC * +	

What modifications must be made to this algorithm to accommodate parenthesis? The answer is little when an opening parenthesis is read, it must be pushed onto the stack. This ensures that an operator symbol appearing after a left parenthesis is pushed onto the stack. When a closing parenthesis is read, all operators up to the first opening parenthesis must be popped from the stack into the postfix string.

Example: Converting (A+B)*C into postfix expression.

S.No.	Symb	Postfix String	Opstk
1	(		(
2	A	A	(
3	+	A	(+
4	B	AB	(+
5	)	AB+	
6	*	AB+	*
7	C	AB+C	*
		AB+C*	

Example: Converting (A+B)*(C-D) into postfix expression.

S.No.	Symb	Postfix String	Opstk

1	(		(
2	A	A	(
3	+	A	(+
4	B	AB	(+
5	)	AB+	
6	*	AB+	*
7	(	AB+	*(
8	C	AB+C	*(
9	-	AB+C	*(-
10	D	AB+CD	*(-
11	)	AB+CD-	*
12		AB+CD-*	

Example: Converting ((A-(B+C))*D)$(E+F) into postfix expression.

S.No.	Symb	Postfix String	Opstk
1	(		(
2	(		((
3	A	A	((
4	-	A	((-
5	(	A	((-(
6	B	AB	((-(
7	+	AB	((-(+
8	C	ABC	((-(+
9	)	ABC+	((-
10	)	ABC+-	(
11	*	ABC+-	(*
12	D	ABC+-D	(*
13	)	ABC+-D*	
14	$	ABC+-D*	$
15	(	ABC+-D*	$(
16	E	ABC+-D*E	$(
17	+	ABC+-D*E	$(+
18	F	ABC+-D*EF	$(+
19	)	ABC+-D*EF+	$
20		ABC+-D*EF+$	

A Program to convert the given infix expression to post expression.

```c
#include<stdio.h>
#include<conio.h>
#include<ctype.h>
void push(char);
char pop( );
int opera(char);
int prio(char);
char stack[20];
int top=-1;
void main( )
{
char inf[10],ch;
int i;
printf("enter infix expression");
scanf("%s",inf);
for(i=0;inf[i]!='\0';i++)
{
if(isalnum(inf[i]))
printf("%c",inf[i]);
else if(opera(inf[i])
{
while(prio(inf[i])<=prio(stack[top]))
{
printf("%c",pop());
                }
push(inf[i]);
}
else if(inf[i]=='(')
push(inf[i]);
else if(inf[i]==')')
{
while((ch=pop())!='(')
{
                        printf("%c",ch);
                }
        }
}
while(top!=-1)
printf("%c",pop());
getch( );
}
```

```c
int opera(char ch)
{
if(ch=='+'||ch=='-'||ch=='*'||ch=='/'||ch=='%')
return(1);
else
return(0);
}
int prio(char ch)
{
switch(ch)
{
case '+':
case '-': return(1);
case '*':
case '/':
case '%':return(2);
default: return(0);
        }
}
void push(char ch)
{
 if(top>=max-1)
{
      printf("stack is full");
}
else
{
top++;
stack[top]=ch;
        }
}
char pop( )
{
 char ch;
 if(top==-1)
 {
printf("stack is empty");
exit(0);
        }
else
{
ch=stack[top];
```

top--;
return(ch);
      }
}

Evaluation of Postfix

A given postfix expression can be evaluated using the following algorithm.

Algorithm:
1. Scan the given postfix expression from left to right.
2. If an operand is found, push it on to the stack.
3. If an operator is found, pop two operands from stack and perform the operation in the order S[top-1] operator S[top]. Push the resultant on to the stack.
4. Repeat the steps 2 and 3 until the right most end is reached.

Example: 345*2%+

Input	output
3	3
3,4	
3,4,5	
*	3,20
2	3.20,2
%	3,0
+	3

Thus , the result of the given postfix expression is 3.

A Program to evaluate the given postfix expression.

```
void push(int);
int pop();
int opera(char);
int stack[10],top=-1;
void main()
{
        int i,x,y;
char post[10];
```

```c
printf("enter any postfix expression");
scanf("%s",post);
for(i=0;post[i]!='\0';i++)
{
if(isdigit(post[i])
{
push(post[i]-48);
            }
else if(opera(post[i])
{
x=pop();
y=pop();
switch(post[i])
{
case '+': push(y+x);
        break;
case '-': push(y-x);
        break;
case '*': push(y*x);
        break;
case '/': push(y/x);
         break;
case '%': push(y%x);
          break;
}
}
}
if(top==0)
{
printf("result=%d",pop());
      }
      getch();
}
      void push(int ele)
{
 if(top>=max-1)
 {
 printf("stack is full");
        }
else
{
                        top++;
```

```c
                stack[top]=ele;
        }
}
int pop()
{
        int ele;
        if(top==-1)
        {
                printf("stack is empty");
                return(-1);
        }
        else
        {
                ele=stack[top];
                top--;
                return(ele);
        }
}
int opera(char ch)
{
        if(ch=='+'||ch=='-'||ch=='*'||ch=='/'||ch=='%')
        return(1);
        else
        return(0);
}
```

Linked Lists

A list refers to a set of items organized sequentially. A linked list is a list of nodes in which each node is represented by a structure. There are different types of linked lists.

Singly Linked

In a singly linked list, each node consists of two fields. One is information field and the other is address fields. It can be represented using a structure as:

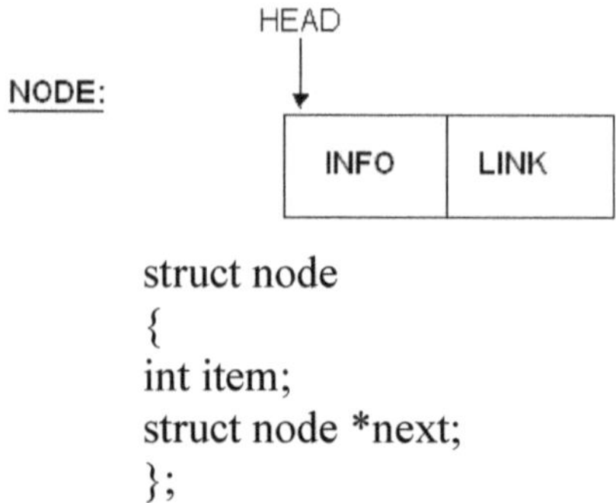


```
struct node
{
int item;
struct node *next;
};
```

Information field consists of the data that has to be stored in that node which may be an integer or float or any other datatype. The address field contains the address of the next node in the list. The address filed of the last nod is always NULL.

Representation:

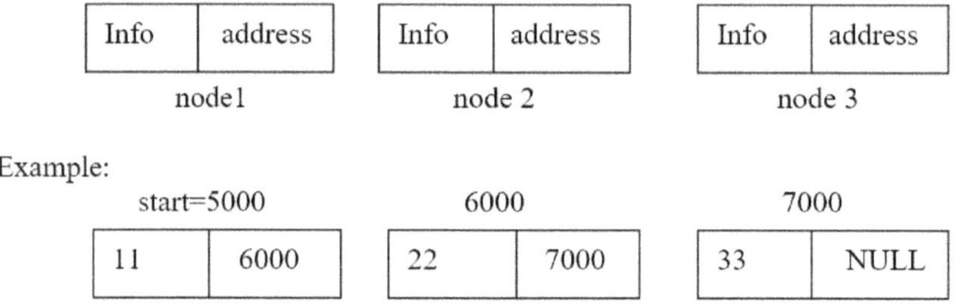

Example:

Possible operations are insertion, deletion, display.

a)   *Insertion:* It is a process of adding a new node to the existing node.

   (i) *At beginning*: To insert any node at the beginning of the list, assign address of the first node to the address field of the new node.

   (ii) *At ending:* To insert any node at the end of the list, assign the new node address to the address field of the last node and make the address field of the new node as NULL.

(iii) *At desired position:* To insert any node at a desired position, the new node address has to be stored in the previous node's address field and the next address has to be stored in new node's address field.

b) Deletion: It is a process of deleting an existing node from the list.
   (i) *At beginning:* First node has to be made NULL and second node is made as start node.
   (ii) *At ending:* Last node has to be made NULL and the address field of prevous to last node is made NULL.
   (iii) *At desired position:* The address field of previous node to the node to be deleted has to be made to store the next node's address field.

c) Display: It is a process of displaying all the elements of the list.

operations

Count( ): Count the number of elements in the list.
Addatbeg(x): Add x to the beginning of the list.
Addatend(x):   Add x at the end of the list.
Insert(k, x): Insert x just after kth element.
Delete(k): Delete the kth element.
Search(x): Return the position of x in the list otherwise return -1 if not found Display( ): Display all elements of the list

Count( )

```
COUNT( )
Temp = Head
Count = 0
While Temp ≠ NULL
       Count = Count +1
       Temp = Link (Temp)
End While
Return Count
End COUNT
```

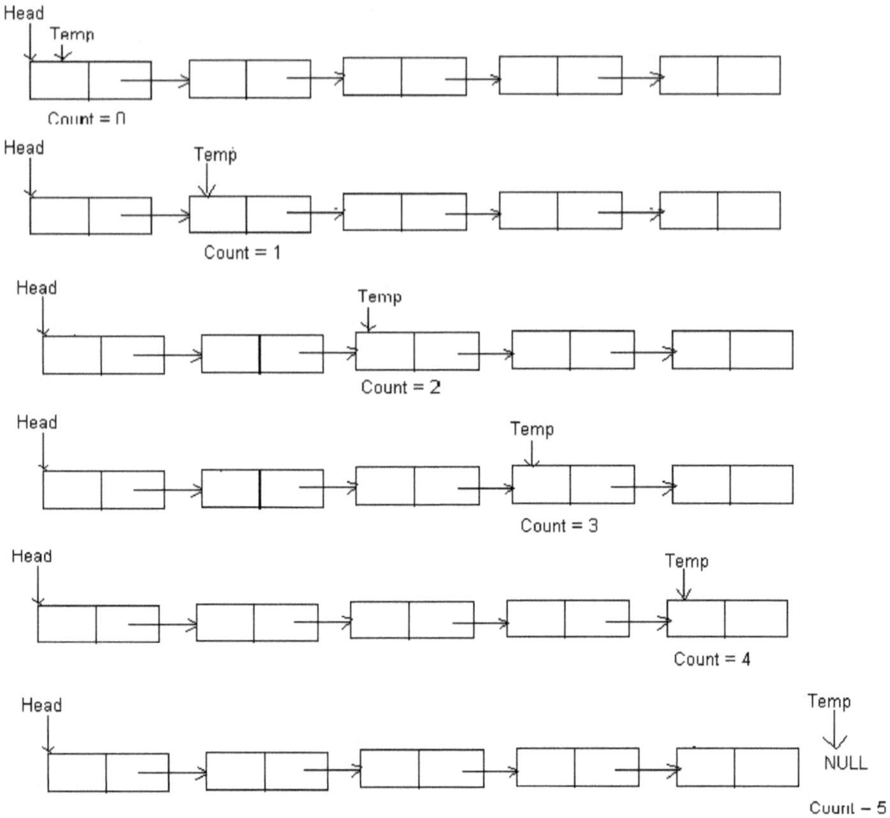

Head
Temp
Count = 0
Head
Temp
Count = 1
Head
Temp
Count = 2
Head
Temp
Count = 3
Head
Temp
Count = 4
Head
Temp
NULL
Count = 5

Addatbeg(x)

Head
NULL
K
New
NULL
Head
K
New

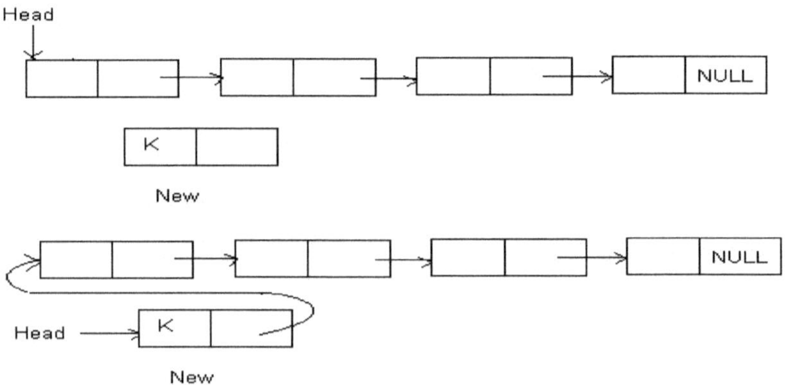

ADDATBEG(K)

Info(New) = K
If Head = NULL
Then
                    Link(New) = NULL
Else
                    Link(New) = Head
Endif
Head = New
End ADDATBEG

Addatend(x)

ADDATEND(X)

If Head = NULL
        Info(Temp) = x
        Link(Temp) = NULL
        Head = Temp
Else
        Temp = Head
        While link(Temp) ≠ NULL
                Temp = link(Temp)
        End Whjle
        Info(New) = x
        Link(New)=NULL
        Link(Temp) = New
Endif
End ADDATEND( )

Insert(k, x)

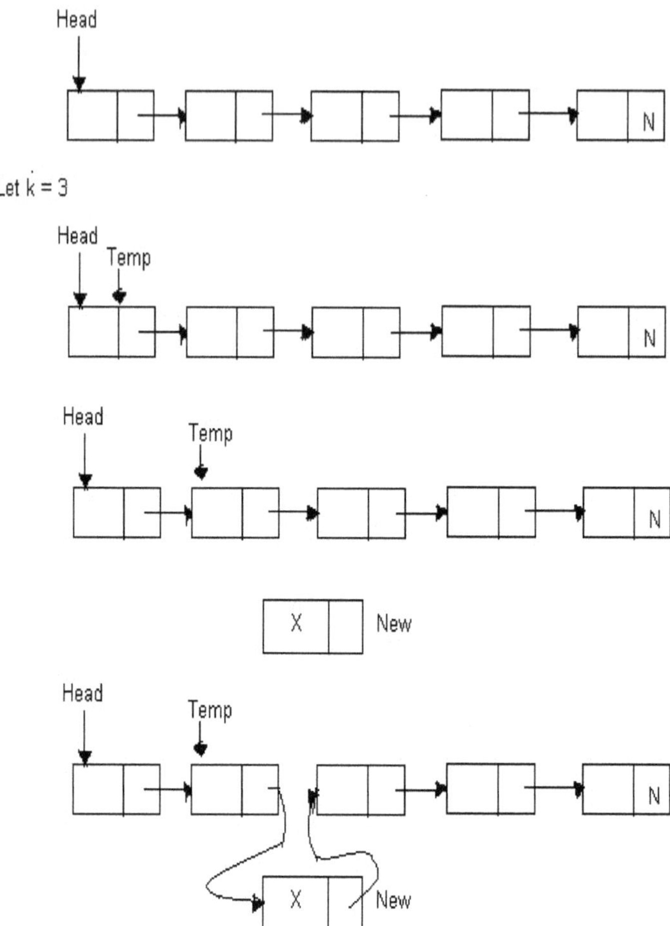

INSERT (k, x)

Temp = Head
I = 1
While I < k-1
        Temp = link(Temp)
        I = I + 1
End While
Info(New) = x
Link(New) = Link(Temp)
Link(Temp) = New
End INSERT( )

Delete (x)

```
DELETE( x )

Temp = Head
While Temp ≠ NULL
        If Info(Temp) = x
        Then
                If Temp = Head
                Then
                        Head = link(Temp)
                Else
                        Link(old) = Link(Temp)
                End If
                Delete Temp
Else
                Old = Temp
                Temp = Link(Temp)
End If
End While
End DELETE( )
```

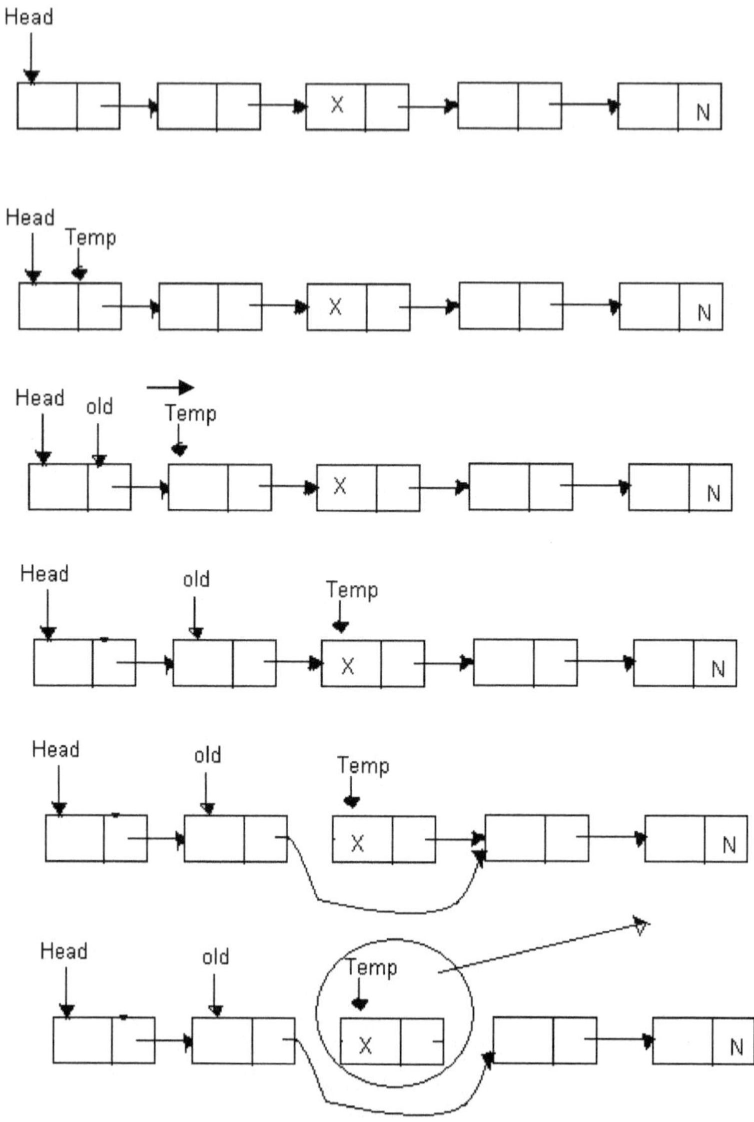

Search(x)
SEARCH(x)

Temp = Head
Count = 1
While Temp ≠ NULL

        If Info(Temp) = x
        Then
                Print count
        End If
        Count = Count + 1
        Temp = Link(Temp)
End While
End SEARCH( )

Display( )

The operation Display( ), displays all the value in each node of the list.
A temporary pointer is created and made to point to Head initially.
Now info part of Temp is printed and Temp is moved to the next node.
This is repeated till the end of the list is reached.

A Program that to perform the following operations on a singly
linked list.
        (a) Creation (b) Insertion (c) Deletion (d) traversal

```c
#include<stdio.h>
#include<conio.h>
 void create(int);
 void insatend(int);
 void insatpos(int,int);
 void delatbeg( );
 void delatend( );
 void delatpos(int);
 void traversal( );
 struct node
 {
  int ele;
  struct node *next;
 };
 struct node *start=NULL;
 void main( )
{
int ch,ele;
printf("1.create 2.insatend 3.insertion at position
4.delatbEg 5.delatend 6.deletion at position 7.traversal");
```

```c
do
{
printf("enter ur choice");
scanf("%d",&ch);
switch(ch)
{
case 1: printf("enter element to be inserted");
        scanf("%d",&ele);
        create(ele);
        break;
case 2: printf("enter element to be inserted");
        scanf("%d",&ele);
        insatend(ele);
        break;


case 3: printf("enter element and position to be
                inserted");
        scanf("%d%d",&ele,&pos);
        insatpos(ele,pos);
        break;
case 4: delatbeg();
        break;
case 5: delatend();
        break;
case 6: printf("enter position to be deleted");
        scanf("%d",&pos);
        delatpos(pos);
        break;
case 7: traversal();
        break;
}
}
while(ch>=1&&ch<=7);
getch( );
        }
    void create(int ele)
{
struct node *temp;
temp=(struct node*)malloc(sizeof(struct node));
temp->ele=ele;
if(start==NULL)
```

```c
{
start=temp;
start->next=NULL;
        }
else
{
temp->next=start;
start=temp;
        }
}
void insatend(int ele)
{
struct node *temp,*p;
temp=(struct node*)malloc(sizeof(struct node));
temp->ele=ele;
if(start==NULL)
{
start=temp;
start->next=NULL;
        }
        else
        {
p=start;
while(p->next!=NULL)
p=p->next;
            p->next=temp;
     temp->next=NULL;
        }
}
void insatpos(int ele,int pos)
{
struct node *temp;
temp=(struct node*)malloc(sizeof(struct node));
temp->ele=ele;
if(start==NULL)
{
if(pos==1)
{
start=temp;
start->next=NULL;
            }
 else
```

```c
printf("insertion is not possible at this position");
        }
      else if (start->next==NULL)
      {
           if(pos==1)
           {
temp->next=start;
start->next=NULL;
start=temp;
}
else if(pos==2)
{
start->next=temp;
temp->next=NULL;
           }
else
printf("insertion is not possible at this position");
}
else
{
int count=0;
struct node *p;
p=start;
while(p!=NULL)
{
p=p->next;
count++;
           }
if(pos<=count+1)
{
if(pos==1)
{
temp->next=start;
start=temp;
              }
else
{
p=start;
for(i=1;i<pos-1;i++)
p=p->next;
temp->next=p->next;
p->next=temp;
```

```c
                }
            }
else
printf("insertion is not possible at this position");
}
}
void delatbeg()
{
struct node *temp;
if(start==NULL)
printf("list is empty");
else if(start->next==NULL)
{
temp=start;
start=NULL;
free(temp);
    }
        else
        {
temp=start;
start=start->next;
free(temp);
        }
}
void delatend()
{
struct node *temp;
if(start==NULL)
printf("list is empty");
else if(start->next==NULL)
{
temp=start;
start=NULL;
free(temp);
    }
else
{
struct node *p;
p=start;
while(p->next->next!=NULL)
p=p->next;
temp=p->next;
```

```c
p->next=NULL;
        free(temp);
      }
}
void delatpos(int pos)
{
struct node *temp,*p;
int count=0;
if(start==NULL)
printf("list is empty");
else if (start->next==NULL)
{
 if(pos==1)
 {
temp=start;
start=NULL;
free(temp);
            }
else
printf("deletion is not possible at this position");
      }
      else
      {
p=start;
while(p!=NULL)
{
p=p->next;
count++;
          }
if(pos<=count)
{
if(pos==1)
{
temp=start;
start=start->next;
free(temp);
          }
               else
               {
for(i=1;i<pos-1;i++)
p=p->next;
temp=p->next;
```

```c
p->next=p->next->next;
free(temp);
                }
            }
else
printf("deletion is not possible at this position");
        }
}
void traversal()
{
struct node*p;
if(start==NULL)
printf("list is empty");
else
{
p=start;
while(p!=NULL)
{
printf("%d\t",p->ele);
p=p->next;
            }
        }
}
```

Doubly Linked List

Doubly linked list: The Doubly linked list is a collection of nodes each
of which consists of three parts namely the data part, prev pointer and
the next pointer. The data part stores the value of the element, the prev
pointer has the address of the previous node and the next pointer has
the value of the next node.

NODE

PREV	DATA	NEXT

In a doubly linked list, the head always points to the first node. The prev pointer of the first node points to NULL and the next pointer of the last node points to NULL.

Operations on a Doubly linked list are,
1. Count the number of elements.
2. Add an element at the beginning of the list.
3. Add an element at the end of the list.
4. Insert an element at the specified position in the list.
5. Delete an element from the list.
6. Display all the elements of the list.

In a doubly linked list, each node consists of three fields: information field, previous address field and next address field. It is represented using structure as follows:

```
struct node
{
struct node *prev;
int item;
struct node *next;
};
```

Possible operations: Insertion, Deletion, Display

Operations

Count( ): Count the number of elements in the list.
Addatbeg(x): Add x to the beginning of the list.
Addatend(x): Add x at the end of the list.
Insert(k, x): Insert x just after kth element.
Delete(k): Delete the kth element.
Search(x): Return the position of x in the list otherwise return -1 if not found
Display( ): Display all elements of the list

a) Insertion:

(i)*At beginning:*
- Address in prev field of first node has to be stored in next field of newly inserted node.
- Prev field of newly inserted node has to be made NULL.
- Prev field of first node should store address of the new node.

(ii)*At ending:*
- next field of last node should store address of new node.
- Prev field of new node should store address of last node.
- Next field of new node should be made NULL.

(iii)*At desired position:*
- New node's prev field should store the address of previous node.
- New node's next field should store the address of next node
- next field of previous node should store the address of new node.
- Prev field of next node should store address of new node.

b) Deletion:

(i)*At beginning:*
- start node has to be made NULL.
- Second node's prev field should store NULL.
- Second node should be made start node.

(ii)*At ending:*
- last node should be made NULL.
- New last node's next field should be made NULL.

(iii)*At desired position:*
- next field of previous element to the element that is to be deleted should contain the address of next element to the element to be deleted.
- Prev field of next element should contain address of previous element to the element to the deleted.

Algorithm:

The operations count( ), Search(x) and Delete(x) are similar to that of the singly linked list.

Addatbeg(x)

ADDATBEG(x)

Info(R) = x
Prev(R) = NULL
Next(R) = head
Prev(head) = R

Head = R
End ADDATBEG( )

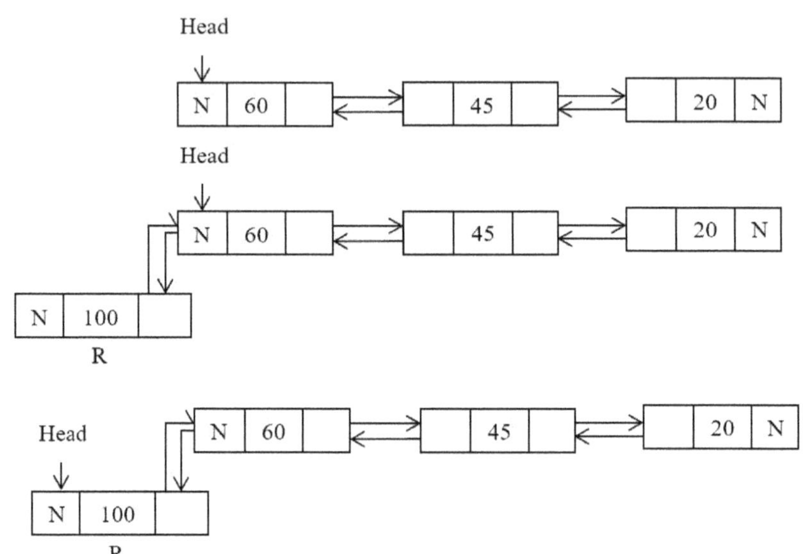

Addatend(x)

ADDATEND(x)

If head = NULL
Then
  Info(R) = x
  Next(R) = NULL
  Prev(R) = NULL
  Head = R
Else
Temp = head
While next(temp) ≠ NULL
   Temp = next(temp)
  End While
Info(R) = x
Next(R) = NULL
Prev(R) = Temp

Next(Temp) = R
End If
End ADDATEND( )

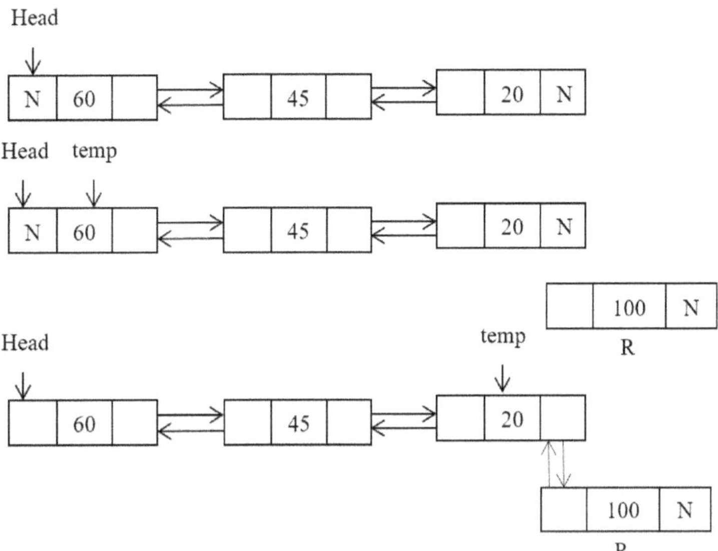

Insert(x, k)

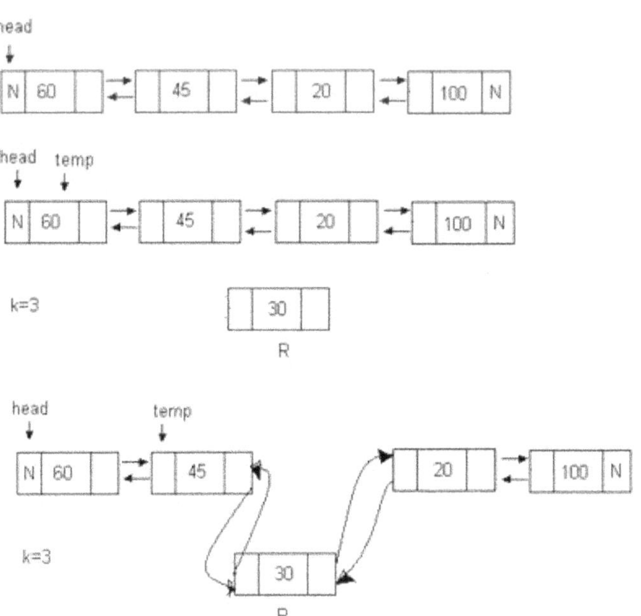

INSERT(x, k)

```
Temp = head
I = 1
While I < k -1
                Temp = next (temp)
                I = I + 1
End while
Next(R) = Next(temp)
Prev(Next(Temp)) = R
Next(Temp) = R
Prev(R) = Temp
End INSERT( )
```

Delete(x)

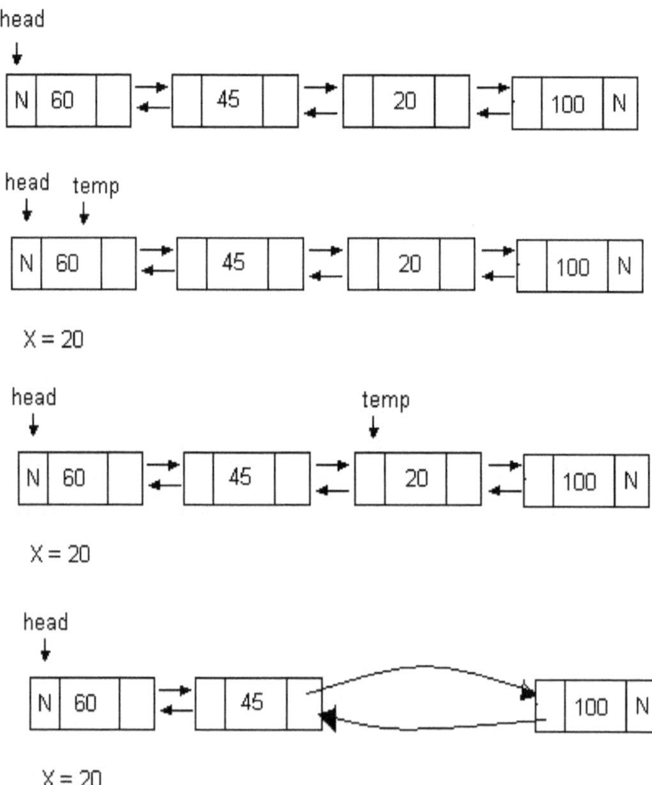

                    DELETE(x)
                    temp = head
                    while temp ≠ NULL
                    if x = info(temp)
                                then
                                        If head = temp
                                        then
                                        Prev(next(temp) = NULL
                                                Head = next(temp)
                                                Delete temp
                                        Else
                                                Prev(next(temp)) =
                    prev(temp)
                                Next(prev(temp))= next(temp)
                                        Delete temp
                                End if
                                     Else
                                Temp = next(temp)
                    End if
                    End while
                    End DELETE( )

A Program to perform the following operations on a doubly linked list.

 (a) Creation (b) Insertion (c) Deletion (d) traversal in both ways

```c
 #include<stdio.h>
#include<conio.h>
void create(int);
void insatend(int);
void insatpos(int,int);
void delatbeg();
void delatend();
void delatpos(int);
void traversal();
void traversalback();
struct node
{
 int ele;
```

```c
struct node *prev;
struct node *next;
};
struct node *start=NULL;
        void main()
{
int ch,ele;
printf("1.create 2.insatend 3.insertion at position
4.delatbeg 5.delatend 6.deletion at position
7.traversal 8.traversalback");
do
{
printf("enter ur choice");
scanf("%d",&ch);
switch(ch)
{
        case 1: printf("enter element to be inserted");
         scanf("%d",&ele);
         create(ele);
         break;
        case 2: printf("enter element to be inserted");
         scanf("%d",&ele);
         insatend(ele);
         break;
        case 3: printf("enter element and position to be
                 inserted");
         scanf("%d%d",&ele,&pos);
         insatpos(ele,pos);
         break;
case 4: delatbeg();
        break;
case 5: delatend();
        break;
        case 6: printf("enter position to be deleted");
         scanf("%d",&pos);
         delatpos(pos);
         break;
case 7: traversal();
        break;
case 8: traversalback();
        break;
        }
```

```c
            }
        while(ch>=1&&ch<=8);
}
void create(int ele)
{
struct node *temp;
temp=(struct node*)malloc(sizeof(struct node));
temp->ele=ele;
if(start==NULL)
{
start=temp;
start->prev=NULL;
start->next=NULL;
        }
        else
        {
temp->next=start;
temp->prev=NULL;
start=temp;
        }
}
void insatend(int ele)
{
struct node *temp,*p;
temp=(struct node*)malloc(sizeof(struct node));
temp->ele=ele;
if(start==NULL)
{
start=temp;
start->prev=NULL;
start->next=NULL;
        }
        else
        {
p=start;
while(p->next!=NULL)
p=p->next;
        temp->prev=p;
        p->next=temp;
        temp->next=NULL;
        }
}
```

```c
void insatpos(int ele,int pos)
{
 struct node *temp;
temp=(struct node*)malloc(sizeof(struct node));
temp->ele=ele;
if(start==NULL)
{
if(pos==1)
{
                                start=temp;
                                start->prev=NULL;
                                start->next=NULL;
                }
                        else
printf("insertion is not possible at this position");
                }
                        else if (start->next==NULL)
                        {
                                if(pos==1)
                                {
                                        temp->next=start;
                                        start->prev=temp;
                                        start=temp;
                                        start->prev=NULL;
                                }
                                else if(pos==2)
                                {
                                        start->next=temp;
                                        temp->prev=start;
                                        temp->next=NULL;
                                }
                                else
printf("insertion is not possible at this position");
                        }
                          else
                          {
                                int count=0;
                                struct node *p;
                                p=start;
                                while(p!=NULL)
                                {
                                        p=p->next;
```

```c
                count++;
        }
    if(pos<=count+1)
    {
        if(pos==1)
            {
                temp->next=start;
                start->prev=temp;
                start=temp;
                start->prev=NULL;
        }
        else
        {

                p=start;
                for(i=1;i<pos-1;i++)
                p=p->next;
                temp->next=p->next;
                p->next->prev=temp;
                p->next=temp;
                temp->prev=p;

        }
    }
    else
                printf("insertion is not possible at this position");
        }
    }
    void delatbeg()
    {
            struct node *temp;
            if(start==NULL)
            printf("list is empty");
            else if(start->next==NULL)
            {
                    temp=start;
                    start=NULL;
                    free(temp);
            }
            else
            {
                    temp=start;
                            start=start->next;
```

```c
                start->prev=NULL;
                free(temp);
        }
}
void delatend()
{
        struct node *temp;
        if(start==NULL)
        printf("list is empty");
        else if(start->next==NULL)
        {
                temp=start;
                start=NULL;
                free(temp);
        }
        else
        {
                struct node *p;
                p=start;
                while(p->next->next!=NULL)
                p=p->next;
                temp=p->next;
                p->next=NULL;
                free(temp);
        }
}
void delatpos(int pos)
{
        struct node *temp,*p;
        int count=0;
        if(start==NULL)
        printf("list is empty");
        else if (start->next==NULL)
        {
            if(pos==1)
            {
                        temp=start;
                        start=NULL;
                        free(temp);
            }
                else
printf("deletion is not possible at this position");
```

```c
            }
          else
          {
              p=start;
              while(p!=NULL)
              {
                      p=p->next;
                      count++;
              }
              if(pos<=count)
              {
                      if(pos==1)
                      {
                              temp=start;
                              start=start->next;
                              start->prev=NULL;
                              free(temp);
                      }
                      else
                      {
                              for(i=1;i<pos-1;i++)
                              p=p->next;
                              temp=p->next;
                              temp->next->prev=p;
                              p->next=p->next->next;
                              free(temp);
                      }
              }
              else
              printf("deletion is not possible at this position");
          }
}
void traversal()
{
        struct node*p;
        if(start==NULL)
        printf("list is empty");
        else
        {
        p=start;
            while(p!=NULL)
          {
```

```
                        printf("%d\t",p->ele);
                        p=p->next;
                  }
            }
      }
      void traversalback()
      {
            struct node *p;
            if(start==NULL)
            printf("list is empty");
            else
            {
                  p=start;
                  while(p->next!=NULL)
                  p=p->next;
                  while(p!=NULL)
                  {
                        printf("%d\t",p->ele);
                        p=p->prev;
                  }
            }
      }
}
```

A Program to implement stack using linked lists.

```
#include<stdio.h>
#include<conio.h>
void push( );
void pop( );
void display( );
struct node
{
int ele;
struct node *next;
}*start;
void main( )
{
int ch;
start=NULL;
do
{
printf("1.Push\n 2.Pop\n 3.Display\n");
```

```c
printf("Enter ur choice");
scanf("%d",&ch);
switch(ch)
{
case 1: push() ;
        break;
case 2: pop( );
        break;
case 3: display( );
        break;
default: printf("Enter choice");
        break;
                }
        }
        while(ch>=1&&ch<=3);
}
void push( )
{
struct node *temp;
temp=(struct node*)malloc(sizeof(struct node));
printf("Enter element to be inserted");
scanf("%d",&temp->ele);
temp->next=start;
start=temp;
}
void pop( )
{
struct node *temp;
if(start==NULL)
{
printf("list is empty");
else
{
temp=start;
printf("Deleted element is %d",temp->ele);
start=start->next;
free(temp);
                }
        }
void display( )
{
struct node *p;
```

```
p=start;
if(start==NULL)
printf("List is empty");
else
{
while(p!=NULL)
{
printf("%d",p->ele);
p=p->next;
        }
    }
}
```

A Program to implement queue using arrays.

```
#define max 20
void enqueue(int);
 int dequeue();
void display();
int queue[max],f=0,r=-1;
void main()
{
        int ele, ch;
        do
        {
printf("1.Enqueue\n 2.Dequeue \n3.Display\n");
                printf("Enter ur choice");
                scanf("%d", &ch);
                switch(ch)
                {
case 1: printf("Enter element to be inserted");
                                scanf("%d",&ele);
                                enqueue(ele);
                                break;
case 2: ele=dequeue();
                                if(ele!=-1)
                        printf("Deleted element is %d",ele);
                                break;
case 3: display();
                                break;
                }
        }
```

```c
        while(ch>=1&&ch<=3);
}
  void enqueue(int ele)
   {
            r++;
             if(r>=max-1)
            printf("queue is full");
            else
             {
        queue[r]=ele;
             }
   }
   int dequeue()
   {
            int ele;
            if(f>r)
             {
                    printf("queue is empty");
             }
            else
             {
                    ele=queue[f];
                    f++;
                    return(ele);
             }
   }
   void display()
   {
   int i;
            if(f>r)
             {
                    printf("queue is empty");
             }
            else
             {
                    for(i=f;i<=r;i++)
                    printf("%d ",queue[i]);
             }
   }
```

Circular Linked List

Logical representation of the circular linked list:

Circular Linked List: Circular linked list is a linked list which consists of collection of nodes each of which has two parts, namely the data part and the link part. The data part holds the value of the element and the link part has the address of the next node. The last node of list has the link pointing to the first node thus making the circular traversal possible in the list.

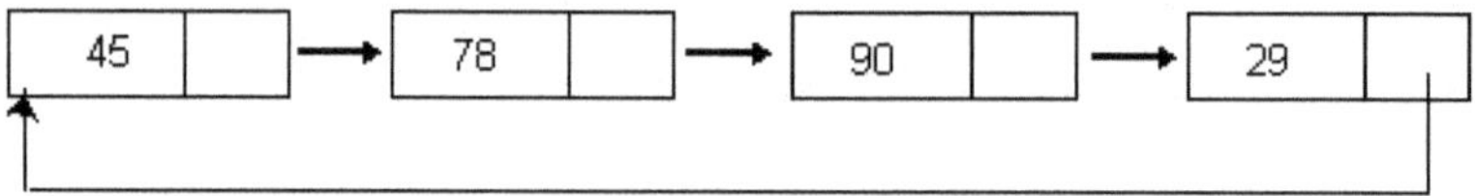

8. Trees and Graphs

Objective

1. Providing the knowledge on Trees and Graphs
2. Able to implement the concepts of trees and graphs
3. Learn the applications of Graph Traversals

This chapter delves into the intricate world of Trees and Graphs, two fundamental data structures that shape the landscape of complex information representation and traversal in programming. Trees, with their hierarchical structure, introduce a paradigm for organizing data in a way that mirrors natural relationships. We'll explore binary trees, AVL trees, and more, unravelling their applications in diverse scenarios, from hierarchical file systems to efficient searching algorithms.

Simultaneously, the narrative extends to Graphs, dynamic structures that capture complex relationships among interconnected entities. Graphs open doors to modelling intricate networks, from social connections to transportation systems. We'll delve into directed and undirected graphs, spanning trees, and algorithms that navigate these structures, illuminating the versatility and power embedded in graph-based representations.

Throughout this exploration, we navigate the realms of hierarchical order and interconnected complexity, understanding how Trees and Graphs become indispensable tools for solving real-world problems in diverse domains. Join the journey into this chapter, where the branches of Trees and the interconnections of Graphs weave a tapestry of structured data representation and algorithmic exploration.

Introduction to Trees

Binary Tree: Binary tree is a tree and each item has two links, one is called left member and another is called right member.

Example:

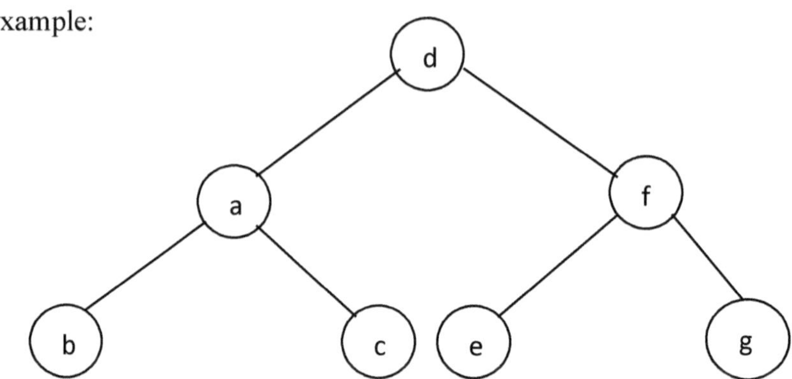

Here d is root of the tree each data item 'a' through 'g' is called a node .

Tree: A tree is a recursive or self repeating data structure and recursive programming techniques are popularly used with trees .

Example:

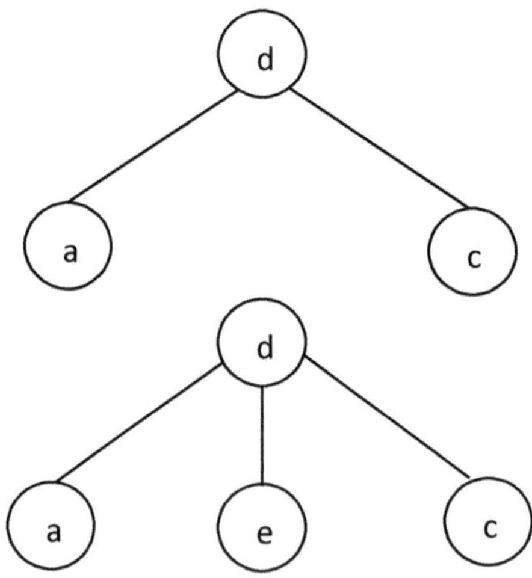

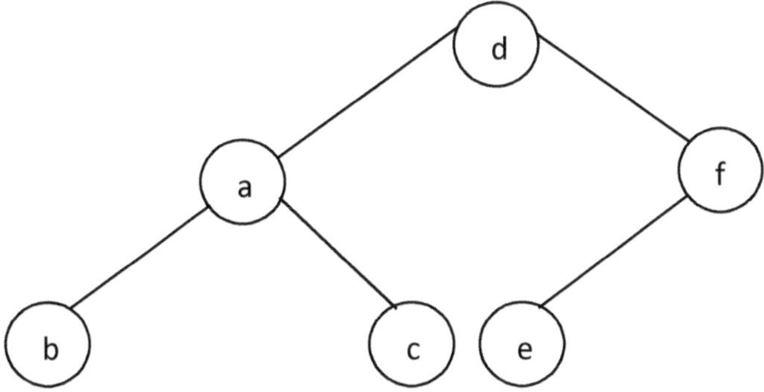

Terminology:

Sub-tree: Any portion of a tree is called a sub tree.

Example:

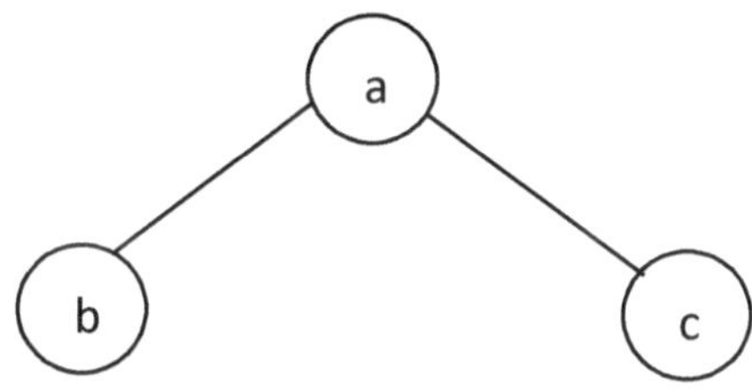

Terminal node: A node that does not have any sub-tee is called as a Terminal node.

Example: a, c, e, g.

Height of Tree: The number of the vertical node positions is called height of that tree.

Example:

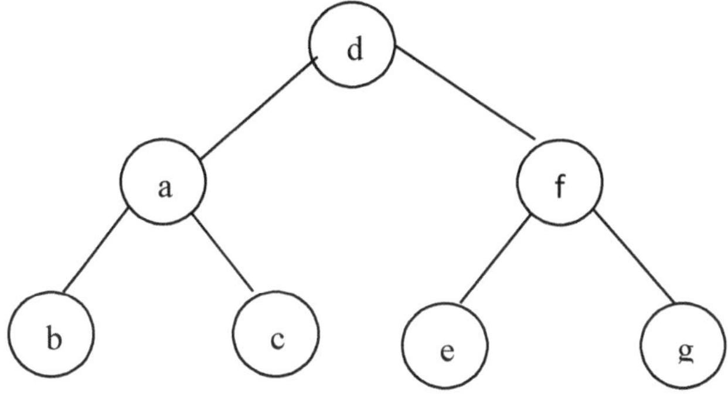

Here height of the tree is 3

Traversals

Tree Traversal: The process of accessing a tree is called tree traversal

.

A tree can be traversal in three ways .. they are,
1. In-Order tree traversal
2. Pre-Order tree traversal
3. post-order tree traversal

Example:,:

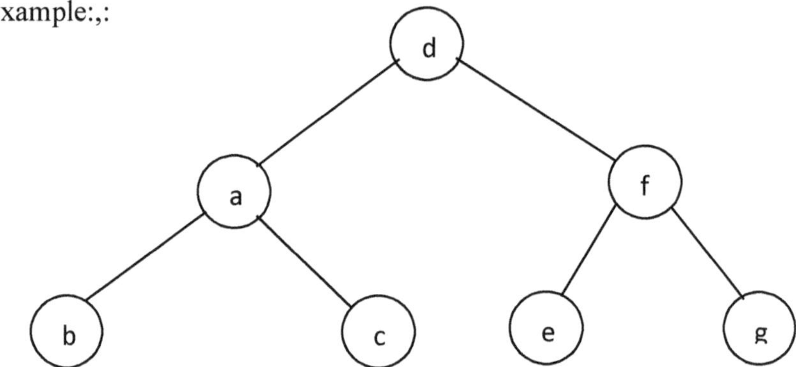

In-Order tree traversal (LOR) : In this ,left subtree is traversed first next root and finally by the right

Sub - tree

Example: for the above figure d-b-a-c-f-e-g.

Pre-Order (OLR): In this , the root is visited first followed by left sub-tree and followed by right sub-tree.

Example: for the above figure a-c-b-e-g-f-d.

Post-Order(LOR): In this, the left sub tree is traversal first followed by the right sub-tree and finally

Followed by root.

Example: for the above figure a-c-b-e-g-f-d.

Actual Representation: The actual representation of a node is given below

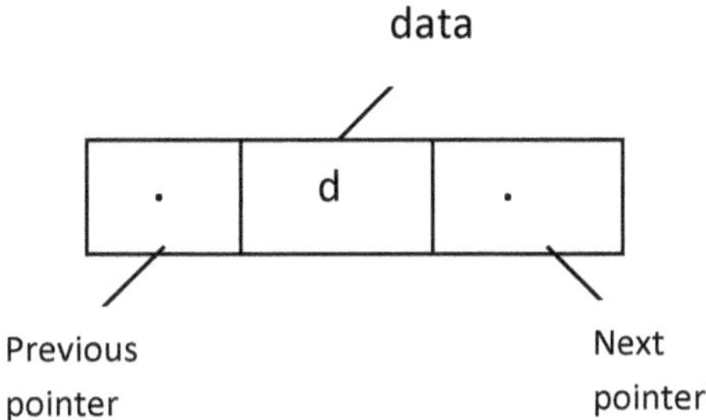

Here…..
Data   : indicates data field
Previous : indicates pointer to the previous field
Next   : indicates pointer to the next field
NOTE : A terminal node can be represented with next and previous pointers zero

Example: the above example can be represented as shown below

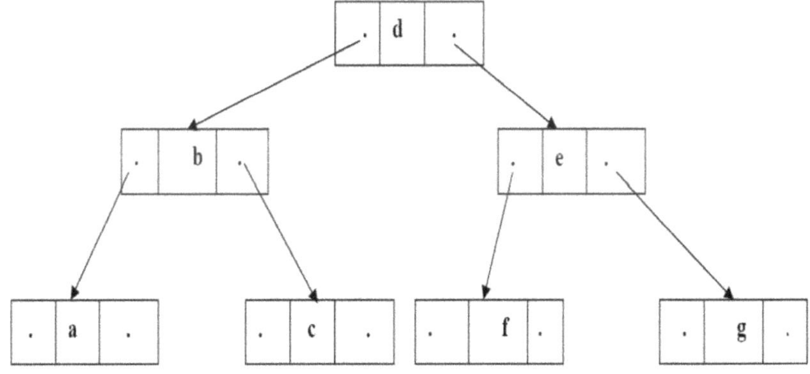

Each node is represented by using structures.

```
Struct tree
{
int number;              /*data to be stored*/
struct tree *left;       /*pointer to the left node*/
struct tree *right;      /*pointer to the right node*/
};
```

A Program that uses functions to perform the following:

(i) Creating a Binary Tree of integers
(ii) Traversing the above tree in preorder, inorder and postorder.

```c
#include<stdio.h>
#include<conio.h>
#include<alloc.h>
typedef struct bt
{
        struct bt *lc;
        int d;
        struct bt *rc;
}node;

void insert(node **,int);
void inorder(node *);
void postorder(node *);
void preorder(node *);
void main( )
{
        node *root=NULL;
        int e,n,i;
        clrscr( );
        printf("\n Enter the Number of Nodes \n");
        scanf("%d",&n);
        printf("\n Enter the Elements \n");
        for(i=1;i<=n;i++)
        {
                scanf("%d",&e);
                insert(&root,e);
        }
        inorder(root);
        postorder(root);
        preorder(root);
}

void insert(node **r,int e)
{
        if(*r==NULL)
        {
                *r=(node *)malloc(sizeof(node));
```

```c
                (*r)->lc=(*r)->rc=NULL ;
                (*r)->d=e;
                return;
        }
        else
        {
                if(e<(*r)->d)
                insert(&((*r)->lc),e);
                else
                insert(&((*r)->rc),e);
        }
}
void inorder(node *r)
{
        if(r!=NULL)
        {
                inorder(r->lc);
                printf("Inorder elements are: %d\n",r->d);
                inorder(r->rc);
        }
        else
        return;
}
void postorder(node *r)
{
        if(r!=NULL)
        {
                postorder(r->lc);
                postorder(r->rc);
                printf("Postorder elements are: %d\n",r->d);
        }
        else
        return;
}
void preorder(node *r)
{
        if(r!=NULL)
        {
                printf("Preorder elements are: %d\n",r->d);
                preorder(r->lc);
                preorder(r->rc);
        }
```

```
            else
            return;
    }
```

Graphs

Definition: "A graph is a set of nodes and a set of arcs".
Nodes are also known as ' vertices ' and ' arcs ' also known as edges.

Example:

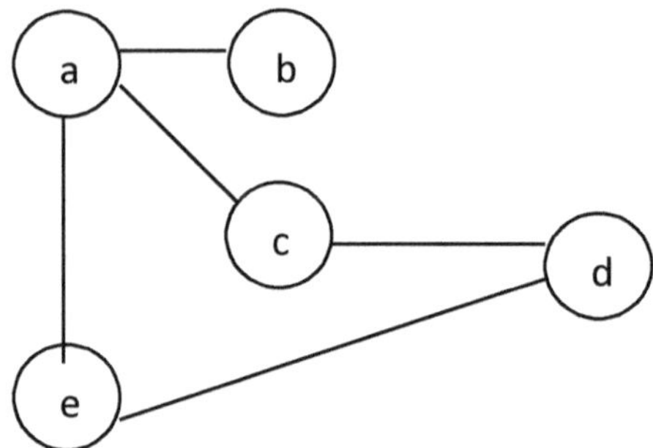

The set of nodes (or) vertices in the above graph is denoted as {A,B,C,D,E}.

Terminology

The set of arcs in the graph is denoted as
    { (A,B),(A,C),(A,D),(A,E),(C,D),(E,D) }

Connected graph: "A graph is connected if here is a path between any two nodes of the graph " i.e.. if we traverse from one node to any other node in the graph, then that graph is called
Connected graph.

Example:

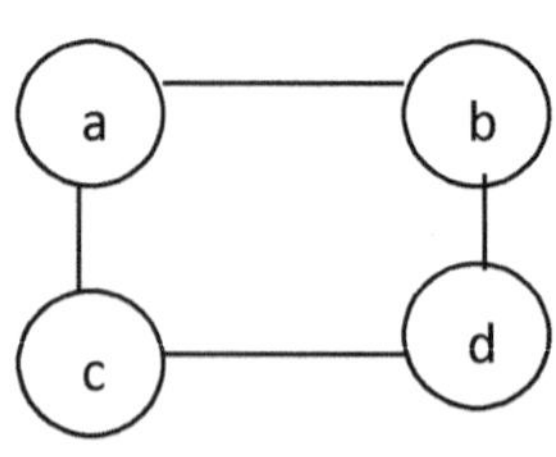

Non connected graph: If we cannot traverse one node to any other node in the graph to that graph is called non connected graph.

Example:

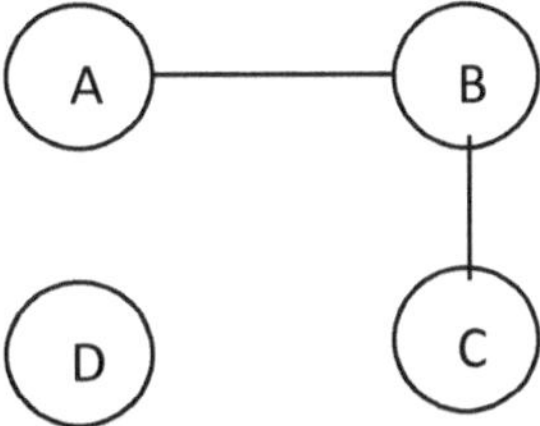

There is no path between A and D ,C and D.

Representation: A graph can be represented as an array (or) as linked list in 'C'. Graph is represented by using two values either '0' or '1' .

  1 – if there is an edge between two nodes.
  0 – if there is no edge between two nodes.

Example:

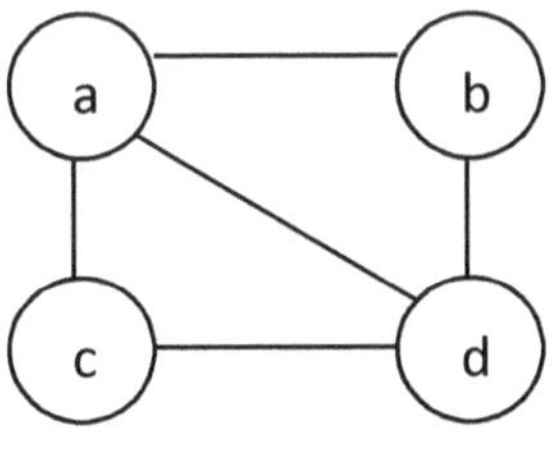

	A	B	C	D
A	0	1	1	1
B	1	0	1	1
C	1	1	0	1
D	1	1	1	0

Traversals

Graph Traversal: Graph traversal is a fundamental operation in graph theory and computer science that involves visiting all the vertices (nodes) and edges (connections) of a graph. There are two main approaches to graph traversal: Depth-First Search (DFS) and Breadth-First Search (BFS).

Depth First Search: First, we select a vertex to traverse a graph and is known as arbitrary vertex, next we will find out all adjacent vertices to the arbitrary vertex. Then we select one node from that set of adjacent vertices. Now, all the vertices that are adjacent to the selected vertex are visited, then another vertex is selected and all of its adjacent vertices are visited and so on. The process continues until all the vertices in the graph are visited. This is known as Depth First Search.

Example:

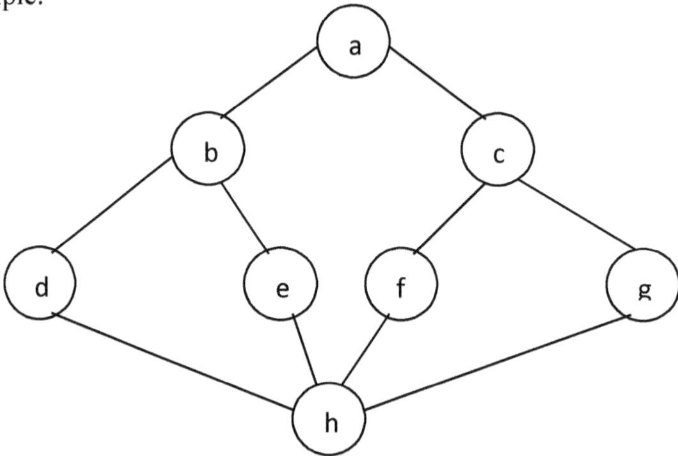

Process:

1. Take 'A' as vertex . arbitrarily .
2. Adjacency vertices to A are B and C .select adjacency as vertex B.
3. Consider adjacent to B are D and E . Then select any i.e.. D.
4. Take adjacent to D are B and H . B is already traversed , then take H.
5. Take adjacent vertices to H are E,F,G. Take any one i.e.. E.

6. Adjacent to E are B and H . these are already traversed then choose another adjacent to H. i.e… F.
7. Adjacent to F are H,C. here select 'C'.
8. Adjacent to C are A,G. A is already traversed and select G

Here all the vertices are visited. Then the sequence to traverse of above graph using Depth first searching
Is " A,B,D,H,E,F,C and G."

Breadth first search (BFS): In this first arbitrary vertex is selected and we need to traverse all the adjacent vertices of the arbitrary vertex. Here the unvisited vertices, which are adjacent the visited vertices are traversed. This process continues until all the vertices in the graph are visited. This process is known as Bread first search.

Example:

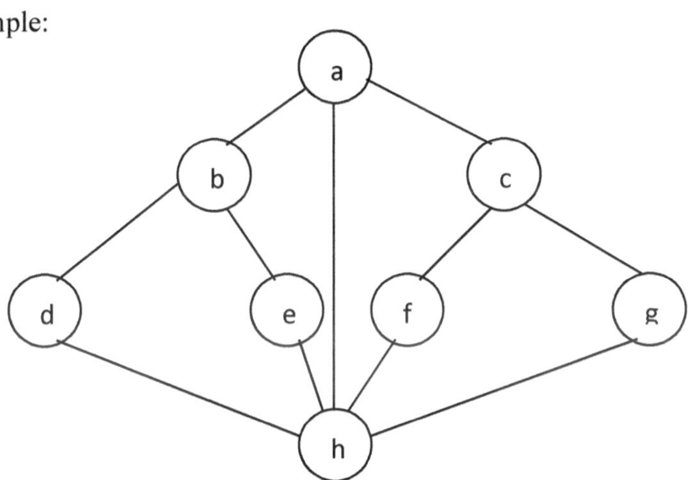

1. Take 'A' as arbitrary vertex.
2. Adjacency vertices to A are B,H,C . Traverse all these vertices.
3. Take 'B' and traverse all the adjacency vertices D and E.
4. Take vertex 'C', traverse unvisited vertices for C are F&G.
5. Then no more unvisited adjacent vertices for the vertices H,D,E,F and G.

The sequence to traverse the above graph by using breadth first search method is A,B,H,C,D,E,F and G.
 The traversal of Breadth first search is shown below.

1.

2.

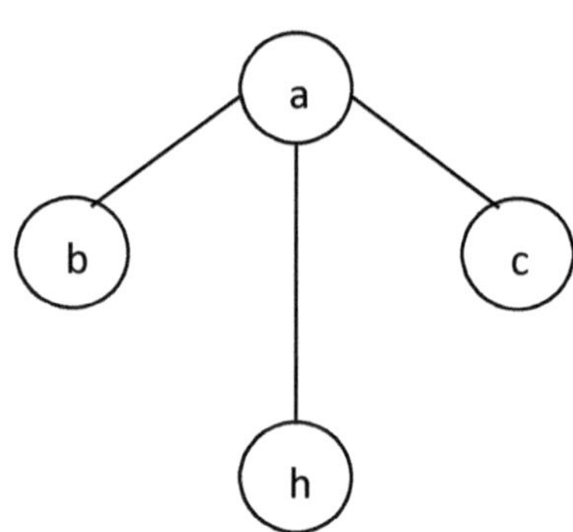

3.

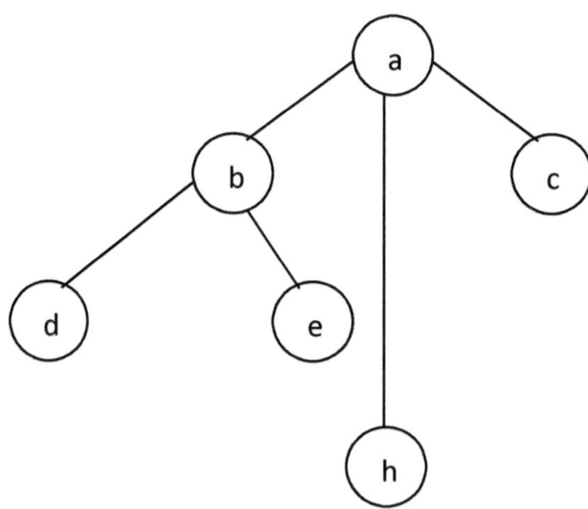

4.

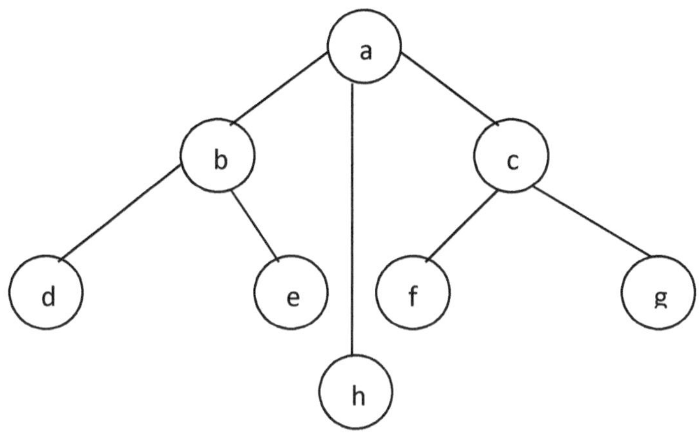

Applications of Graph Traversals

Graph traversal algorithms have a wide range of applications, from finding paths and connectivity in networks to determining reachability and discovering the structure of complex relationships. These algorithms are instrumental in solving real-world problems such as:

Network Routing: Graph traversal is fundamental in determining the most efficient paths in networks, whether it's for data packets in computer networks or optimizing transportation routes in logistics. Social Network Analysis: In social networks, graph traversal helps uncover relationships, identify influencers, and understand the overall structure of connections between individuals or entities.

Web Crawling: Search engines use graph traversal to navigate the vast web. Web crawlers employ algorithms to systematically traverse web pages, indexing and cataloging information for efficient search results.

Shortest Path Finding: Graph traversal algorithms like Dijkstra's or Bellman-Ford are crucial for finding the shortest paths between nodes, applicable in transportation, logistics, and network optimization.

Recommendation Systems: Graph traversal assists in building recommendation systems, identifying related items or interests based on the connections between users and their preferences.

Game Development: In gaming, graph traversal is employed for pathfinding algorithms, determining the best routes for characters or entities within the game environment.

Dependency Resolution: Software and project management utilize graph traversal to resolve dependencies between different modules or components, ensuring a systematic and efficient build process.

Robotics and Autonomous Vehicles: Graph traversal plays a crucial role in path planning for robots and autonomous vehicles, enabling them to navigate through dynamic environments efficiently.

Circuit Analysis: Electrical engineers use graph traversal to analyze circuits, identifying paths, loops, and connections to optimize electrical systems.

Biological Network Analysis: Graph traversal is applied in the analysis of biological networks, such as protein-protein interaction networks, to understand the relationships and functions of biological entities.

In essence, the applications of graph traversal are far-reaching, contributing to the efficiency and optimization of systems in fields ranging from technology and logistics to social sciences and biology. The ability to uncover hidden patterns and relationships within complex networks makes graph traversal an indispensable tool in solving a myriad of real-world problems.

www.ingramcontent.com/pod-product-compliance
Lightning Source LLC
Chambersburg PA
CBHW041307120726
48005CB00014B/1896